HOW CAN I EVER AFFORD CHILDREN?

Wiley Personal Finance Solutions

HOW CAN I EVER AFFORD CHILDREN?

Money Skills for New and Experienced Parents

BARBARA HETZER

JOHN WILEY & SONS, INC.

New York • Chichester • Weinheim • Brisbane • Singapore • Toronto

Copyright © 1998 by Barbara Hetzer. All rights reserved.
Published by John Wiley & Sons, Inc.

Published simultaneously in Canada.

This publication is designed to provide accurate and authoritative information in
regard to the subject matter covered. It is sold with the understanding that the
publisher is not engaged in rendering legal, accounting, or other professional
services. If legal advice or other expert assistance is required, the services of a
competent professional person should be sought.

Designations used by companies to distinguish their products are often claimed
by trademarks. In all instances where the author or publisher is aware of a claim,
the product names appear in Initial Capital letters. Readers, however, should
contact the appropriate companies for more complete information regarding
trademarks and registration.

Library of Congress Cataloging-in-Publication Data:

Hetzer, Barbara.
    How can I ever afford children? : money skills for new and
experienced parents / by Barbara Hetzer.
        p.   cm.—(The Wiley personal finance solutions series)
    Includes index.
    ISBN 0-471-23911-9 (pbk.)
    1. Parents—United States—Finance, Personal.   2. Saving and
investment—United States.   I. Title.   II. Series: Wiley personal
finance solutions.
    HG179.H4533   1998
    332.024'0431—dc21   98-13647

To Alex, Jonathan, and Kate—three perfectly wonderful
reasons why this book needed to be written

CONTENTS

ACKNOWLEDGMENTS

W armest thanks to all who contributed to the research needed for this book, especially Noreen Dieg, an ace accountant (and a dear friend) who helped decipher some tax questions; Hope Feinglass, another financial whiz who drafted several easy-to-understand calculations; Brigid O'Connor, whose new "perspectives" from the Institute of Certified Financial Planners always seemed to hit my in-box just when I needed them; the adoption and surrogacy law offices of Diane Michelsen; Patrick Purtill of the National Council for Adoption; Jayna Nagle of the Insurance Information Institute; Virginia Bueno of the American Council of Life Insurance; and the many associations and organizations across the country which gather data on every group imaginable, from plastic surgeons and children with birth defects to nurse-midwives and parents of twins.

I'd also like to thank the other people who made this book possible. The group at Cape Cod Compositors crossed every "t," found every dangling modifier, and even double-checked my arithmetic. At John Wiley & Sons, Associate Managing Editor Michael Detweiler deftly shuttled my manuscript through the production process; and Editor Debra Wishik Englander offered encouragement, insightful guidance, and some mother-to-mother advice every step of the way. It's been a pleasure, as always, working with such a staff.

INTRODUCTION

I remember telling a close friend of mine that I was having a third child. She didn't say anything. Instead, she just sort of breathed out a long, meaningful "Oooooh!" At first, I wasn't sure if she thought I was crazy, stupid, or blessed with the patience of a saint. But a few more minutes into the conversation and I soon found that my stature had risen dramatically in my friend's eyes. If I was having a third child, then I must be doing rather well *financially* to afford such a brood. Of course, I wasn't about to burst her bubble. She didn't need to know that my checking account that month would barely cover the mortgage, car insurance, and telephone bill.

What *does* it take to raise a child (or two or three) these days? Besides the basics like love, patience, and a sense of humor, you'll need cash—and plenty of it. Some parents (like my fabled friend above) think a small fortune is necessary to afford the cost of karate lessons, summer camp, and those adorable Gap outfits. Even our very own government estimates that a middle-income family spends just $149,820 to bring up a child from birth to age 18.

Neither of these extremes seems right to me. The government figures don't include extras like a personal computer and private tutoring for the SATs, lost wages for a stay-at-home parent, or the biggest budget-wrecker of them all: the cost of a college degree. My friend's assumption seems equally unreasonable. Plenty of people have babies each year, and not all of them have the resources of a Bill Gates.

Certainly, kids are expensive. Just being pregnant is an expensive proposition. Your medical bills can easily exceed $10,000—and that's assuming you don't run into any complications or have trouble conceiving a child in the first place. College tuition is a killer: In 1996, the average cost per year for a private four-year college was nearly $13,000. Plus, there are all those "little" expenses along the way like braces, bar mitzvah parties, and ice skating lessons that can really add up.

The more children you welcome into the world, the higher you can expect your tab to run. The traditional wisdom about economies of scale, unfortunately, doesn't really apply to families (not enough to make that much of a difference anyway). And, if you're like most parents, you may feel that nothing is too good for your son or daughter, even though you probably don't have the resources to give them everything you'd like.

Still, like most other undertakings, parenthood is manageable—if you anticipate some of the costs ahead of time and plan carefully for both short- and long-term goals. It's the unexpected curveballs, generally, that are catastrophic. In the 14 chapters that follow, you'll find a workable blueprint to help you meet some of the financial challenges that you face as a parent.

I've broken down the expenses you'll encounter over the first 18 years of your child's life, everything from the major bills like college to more modest expenses including music lessons and summer camp. I've addressed the everyday-but-often-overlooked choices that are involved. Do you buy the house of your dreams, even though the school district is only so-so? How do you choose your child's guardian, and which type of child care is best? When do children need a Social Security number, and how do you get a birth certificate? I've also included information about some special situations. How do you plan your estate, for instance, if your child is mentally handicapped? When should you put savings in your child's name? And so on.

As a parent, you must make an overwhelming number of financial decisions, often with little or no money on hand. Some items you'll have to pay top dollar for, even if it means borrowing the funds to do so. Other expenses you'll simply have to economize on, or skip outright. Throughout the book, I've included savings tips wherever possible. The "At a Glance" figures are work sheets that are meant to give you a quick estimate of how much you can expect to spend on a particular item—baby gear, for instance, or infertility treatment. Use these work sheets to evaluate your personal situation and determine what you should do.

You won't find all of the answers in this one book, of course. That's why "For More Info"—organizations, books, and other resources that offer more detailed information—has been included at the end of each chapter.

Still worried about how you're going to afford your kids? Stop panicking—and start reading. With proper planning, you can manage your financial responsibilities as a parent in ways that won't keep you pacing the floors at night. Besides, now's the time to catch up on your rest. You'll lose enough sleep once the little one arrives.

CHAPTER ONE

$

The Business of Birth

Kids drain your cash flow—almost from the moment they're conceived. Long before you have to fret about funding college, summer camp, or even that trip to Disney World, you'll first have to bring your little bundle of joy into the world. And that's an expense in itself. The stork, unfortunately, doesn't just drop off your baby gratis anymore. With prenatal care stressed these days from as early as the sixth week of pregnancy, the first expenses you'll probably face as a parent will be the medical bills incurred in the conception, gestation, and birth of your child.

How much you'll pay, and how much you'll have to pay in advance of your child's birth, will depend on whom you choose to deliver your baby; whether the birth takes place in a hospital, a birthing center, or the back of a taxicab; and what kind of insurance plan, if any, both you and your spouse have and how much of these medical expenses will be covered.

Ideally, you should shop for maternity care that best meets your needs—regardless of the price. Unfortunately, however, the high cost of health care will inevitably play into your decision. For a prenatal and delivery program that won't put you into debt, you'll probably have to tailor a childbirth program to your budget.

DOCTOR OR MIDWIFE?

The first expense you'll have to evaluate is the doctor's fee. Many doctors charge a flat fee that includes prenatal visits, delivery, and, frequently, a follow-up visit six weeks after delivery. That fee varies, depending on where you live and if you deliver vaginally or by *cesarean section* (C-section). (See Figure 1.1.) Generally, that fee does not include routine lab work, such as urinalysis and blood tests for protein and sugar levels, nor more elaborate tests, such as a sonogram or an amniocentesis. (See Figure 1.2.)

You don't need a doctor to deliver your baby, of course. Many women who have low-risk pregnancies opt for a certified nurse-midwife instead. Physicians' fees for a normal pregnancy average $2,740 nationwide; those of nurse-midwives run about the same. Still, a nurse-midwife will generally cost you less than a medical doctor because she uses less high-tech equipment (which is billed separately) and focuses more on the natural aspect of childbirth.

Which practitioner is right for you? That depends on the type of pregnancy you have, and the type of birth experience you want. If yours is a high-risk pregnancy—you're carrying triplets, let's say, or you're a diabetic—you'll probably want a medical doctor. But if you're healthy and you want a low-tech, less "medical" birth experience, pick a nurse-midwife. To make the best choice for you and your baby, consider the following:

OBSTETRICIAN

Obstetricians deliver four out of five babies born in the United States. All licensed obstetricians are medical doctors

FIGURE 1.1 WHAT PRICE PREGNANCY?

The cost of having a baby varies widely, depending on the area of the country you live in and whether your baby is born vaginally or by cesarean section. The physicians' charges cited below include prenatal and delivery charges.

GEOGRAPHIC REGION	VAGINAL DELIVERY			CESAREAN DELIVERY		
	HOSPITAL	PHYSICIAN	TOTAL	HOSPITAL	PHYSICIAN	TOTAL
New England	$3,760	$3,160	$6,920	$7,060	$4,480	$11,540
Middle Atlantic	$4,370	$3,980	$8,350	$7,580	$5,460	$13,040
East North Central	$3,600	$2,310	$5,910	$6,750	$3,480	$10,230
West North Central	$3,490	$2,150	$5,640	$6,520	$3,150	$9,670
South Atlantic	$3,550	$2,940	$6,490	$6,760	$4,430	$11,190
East South Central	$3,310	$2,190	$5,500	$5,850	$2,920	$8,770
West South Central	$3,380	$2,340	$5,720	$6,290	$3,590	$9,880
Mountain	$3,240	$2,290	$5,530	$7,010	$3,910	$10,920
Pacific	$3,980	$2,740	$6,720	$8,350	$4,540	$12,890

Source: Reprinted with permission from Health Insurance Association of America, *Source Book of Health Insurance Data 1996.* Data represents only Metropolitan Life claims.

FIGURE 1.2 TESTING, TESTING, TESTING

Whether you use an obstetrician, family practitioner, or nurse-midwife, their prenatal and delivery fees generally don't include all of the testing that is required these days. Expect to pay extra for the following tests:

TEST	AVERAGE COST
Urinalysis	$40
Blood tests	$95
Sonogram	$225
Glucose tolerance	$100
Alpha-fetoprotein (AFP) screening	$125
Amniocentesis	$900

who have at least three years of specialty training in pregnancy, labor, and delivery. Most are board-certified, which means they have received postgraduate training in their field. (That's no guarantee that he or she is a good doctor, of course, but it's generally a good sign that a doctor is up-to-date on procedures, theories, and so forth.) Some are also fellows of their medical specialty societies. If your obstetrician puts FACOG after her name, for instance, it means that she's a fellow of the American College of Obstetricians and Gynecologists.

You can verify your doctor's credentials by calling the American Board of Medical Specialties at 800-776-2378. (You can also contact the American Board of Obstetrics and Gynecology, but you must put your request in writing and include a $25 processing fee: 2915 Vine Street, Dallas, TX 75204; 214-871-1619.) If your doctor is a doctor of osteopathy rather than an MD, you can contact the American Osteopathic Board of Obstetrics and Gynecology to find out if he or she is board-eligible: 1000 East 53d Street, Chicago, IL

60615; 773-947-4632. Put your request in writing and include a $25 processing fee. Or you can call the American Osteopathic Association at 800-621-1773 to verify that a doctor is board-certified. Osteopaths are fully licensed physicians and surgeons, too, but they take a more holistic approach to care.

Why do so many women choose an obstetrician to deliver their babies? If you have already established a trusting relationship with your gynecologist, and your gynecologist is also an obstetrician, you'll probably want to stick with him or her now that you're going to have a baby. (Not all gynecologists maintain an obstetric practice, but many do.) Plus, many women simply like the security of using a specialist. Should any complication arise, the doctor can handle it.

QUESTIONS TO ASK AN OBSTETRICIAN:

- How many cesarean sections do you perform annually? (How many vaginal births?)
- What procedures do you routinely administer during delivery? IVs? Fetal monitoring? Episiotomy?
- Do you encourage natural childbirth?
- At what stage of labor do you administer drugs?
- When do you feel it's necessary to induce labor?
- How frequently have you used forceps or a vacuum extractor in the past year? When would you resort to such methods?

FAMILY PRACTITIONER

The *family practitioner* is a relative newcomer to the obstetrics scene. Basically, he or she is an updated version of the old-fashioned family doctor who took care of you and your kid brother as well as your mother and father. Like an obstetrician, this doctor has three years of training following medical school, but only about three months of that training has to be in obstetrics and gynecology. The focus is "primary care." Some pregnant women like the continuity of care with this type of physician. It's a doctor you already know and trust. He's your internist, your gynecologist—and now your obstetrician. Once he has delivered your baby, a family practitioner can then switch hats and become the baby's pediatrician.

Most family practitioners charge roughly the same as an obstetrician to deliver a baby. To verify this doctor's credentials, contact the American Board of Family Practice: 2228 Young Drive, Lexington, KY 40505-4294; 606-269-5626. You must put your request in writing and include a $25 processing fee.

QUESTIONS TO ASK A FAMILY PRACTITIONER:

- How much of your practice is currently devoted to obstetrics?
- How many babies have you delivered in the past year?
- Were any births complicated?
- Were any of the pregnancies considered high-risk?
- Why, and when, would you refer me to a specialist?

MIDWIFE

Certified nurse-midwives specialize in the prenatal care of healthy women with low-risk pregnancies. They can deliver a baby (provided it's a normal, uncomplicated delivery) and offer postpartum care to both the mother and the newborn.

Only 5.2% of all births were attended by nurse-midwives in 1994 (the latest year for which the records are available). But the number has increased every year since 1975. The five thousand or so certified nurse-midwives in the United States today are registered nurses who have completed at least one year of obstetric training in an approved graduate midwifery program and have passed the national certification examination given by the American College of Nurse-Midwives.

Contrary to what you might think, nurse-midwives don't offer second-class care. The majority of them attend births in hospitals or birth centers, not at home. And most work with a physician, who will take over in case of an emergency or complications. Over the years, study after study has documented the safety and effectiveness of midwifery care. Most recently, researchers at the University of Washington studied 1,300 low-risk pregnant women and found that the patients of nurse-midwives had cesarean section rates of only 8.8%, compared to 13.6% for obstetricians and 15.1% for family physicians.

Lay midwives, on the other hand, aren't licensed or formally trained in obstetrics. Much of their experience is hands-on. A handful of states prohibit lay midwives from practicing. The rest are rather vague on this point: They have no specific laws pertaining to the subject of lay midwives. Why would you go this rather risky route? It's cheaper. Lay midwives charge as little as $1,000. Or, perhaps you simply feel that doctors and hospitals intervene too much in this natural phenomenon called birth, and you want to give birth at home. Most doctors and certified nurse-midwives won't deliver a baby at home anymore. But lay midwives will. In fact, those are the kinds of births that they attend predominantly.

QUESTIONS TO ASK A CERTIFIED NURSE-MIDWIFE:

- Are you certified by the American College of Nurse-Midwives?

- Are you employed by a hospital or a physician's practice?

- Where do most of the births that you attend take place?
- What happens if complications occur during the course of pregnancy or during labor?
- What procedures, such as an episiotomy, are you certified to perform?
- Are you permitted by law to write prescriptions?

FURTHER CONSIDERATIONS

Once you've decided which type of health professional you want to deliver your child, you'll need to find some likely candidates. The following are good sources:

Personal recommendations. Ask your family doctor, your gynecologist (if he or she doesn't do deliveries), and friends and family members (especially those who've recently had babies).

The county medical society. This group should be able to supply a list of names of doctors who deliver babies as well as some information on their training, specialities, board certification, and type of practice.

The American College of Nurse-Midwives. The association's toll-free practice locator line (888-MIDWIFE) will help you find a certified nurse-midwife in your area. You can also check out its Web site—www.midwife—for more information.

Childbirth education programs. Often, these are a good source for parents-to-be, especially if you want a professional who espouses natural childbirth. If you're a breastfeeding advocate, you might try your local La Leche League, too.

Your local hospital. If a nearby hospital boasts a birthing room or an adjacent birthing center that you like, ask for the names of the attending physicians or midwives.

Doctors and midwives generally want their fee up front, before the baby is born. They often expect that payment *in full* by the seventh or eighth month. Sometimes, the practitioner will let you pay just the part not covered by insurance—the 20% or so not covered under a typical indemnity plan, plus your deductible—but you generally must provide an estimate from the insurance company on what they're going to pay. Other doctors and midwives insist that you pay the entire bill now and then get reimbursed from the insurance company. That can be a costly proposition.

When I was pregnant with my second son, my obstetrician insisted that his $6,000 bill be paid by the end of my eighth month. My husband and I were a bit strapped for cash at the time so we kept putting it off. Ultimately, we never had to pay it. I gave birth six and a half weeks early— about two and a half weeks shy of the payment due date— so I just paid the deductible and copayment and filed my insurance claim for the rest. While I obviously wouldn't recommend going into early labor to avoid paying your doctor bill, I wouldn't rush to pay that bill when you're three months pregnant, either. You could go into early labor like me, or miscarry in your fourth month, or, well, you just never know. Hold onto your money until the absolute last moment. And, before you make any payment, make sure you understand what the fee includes—and doesn't include.

Ask the following questions of the doctor or midwife you've selected to deliver your child:

- What is your fee?
- What exactly is included in that fee? All prenatal visits? What about a postpartum checkup?
- Does your fee assume it will be a vaginal birth? If so, how much more does a cesarean birth cost?

- Are there any additional tests, such as amniocentesis, or lab work not included in that fee? How much will those tests cost? Do you expect to be paid up front for them?
- Does insurance generally cover your fees?
- When do you expect payment?
- Will you require me to pay the entire bill up front and wait for reimbursement from my insurance company? Or, can I pay just the portion of your bill that my insurance won't cover?

THE BIRTH SETTING

Paying the doctor or midwife to deliver your baby is only part of the cost. You have to give birth *someplace* and, unless you've decided to give birth at home, you have to pay for the use of that facility.

Most births today take place in hospitals, which are equipped with the latest equipment to deal with almost any medical emergency. Hospitals generally charge a baseline fee for a birth (see Figure 1.1), which varies depending on the region of the country and whether it is a C-section or a vaginal delivery. (Hospital charges are steeper for a C-section because more time is needed to recuperate; the hospital stay is five days rather than the typical two days with a vaginal birth.) Also included in that hospital fee are nursery charges for the baby once he or she is born. If the baby needs more than routine care, such as a brief stay in the intensive care unit, you'll be charged extra.

Often, your hospital bill will be higher if you choose a doctor rather than a nurse-midwife. Doctors simply use more procedures and equipment, all of which cost more and are tacked onto your hospital bill. That epidural may ease your contractions, but it'll cost you about $900. Midwives, on the other hand, use 12.2% fewer resources than doctors, according to a recent study by the University of Washington.

A hospital isn't the only place your baby can be delivered these days, however. Many parents opt for *birth centers*, which are staffed by midwives predominantly, and offer a more homey setting. The difference in cost can be significant. According to the National Association of Childbearing Centers, vaginal births in birthing centers cost $3,241, on average, in 1995; an average vaginal birth in a hospital, by contrast, cost $6,378.

The trouble is, the choice of hospital or birth center is restricted to where your doctor or midwife has privileges. (Obviously, you'll want to keep this in mind when shopping for your health practitioner.) And, if you want to give birth at home, it may be even more problematic. You'll have to find a doctor (almost impossible these days) or midwife who's willing to deliver the child at your home. Ultimately, most parents choose the health practitioner first—and the facility becomes a secondary consideration. But, if you have your heart set on a certain type of birth experience, you should familiarize yourself with these available options, and their advantages and disadvantages:

The *hospital delivery room* offers the most security. Should complications develop during delivery, the technology and a team of doctors and nurses are on hand to deal with it immediately. In recent years, the conventional maternity ward—complete with bright lights, cold metal furnishings, and loads of machinery—has slowly been replaced by warmer, homier *hospital birthing rooms*. With soft lighting, curtains at the window, a rocking chair, and a comfortable bed, these birthing rooms look and feel like a motel room. In most cases, you can labor, deliver, and recover in this same room. Afterward, you'll generally be moved, however, to another private or semiprivate room for the duration of your hospital stay.

Visit the hospital well before your baby is due. If possible, ask a hospital representative the following questions:

- Will I be using a birthing room? (Some hospitals have a limited supply of these. It may depend on how many babies are being delivered that day.)
- Will I be hooked up to a fetal monitor once I'm admitted? Or can I move around freely during labor?
- Can my husband attend the birth? Any other family members?
- After the birth, will I be sharing a room with another mother?
- Do you offer childbirth classes?
- What percentage of women have episiotomies?
- Who administers anesthesia? How often is it used?
- What's the cesarean section rate for the hospital?

Birth or *maternity centers* are a cross between hospital births and home births. They provide a homelike setting, but there's some high-tech equipment on hand for emergencies. Certified nurse-midwives provide the bulk of the care, but obstetric and pediatric doctors are generally on 24-hour call, as needed. Some birth centers are actually based in hospitals; others are freestanding units. All are affiliated with a nearby hospital, however, should serious complications arise during a delivery that require hospital care.

A birth center will cost you about one-half the price of a hospital because you generally stay for only one day. In some cases, you can bring your baby home hours after giving birth. Finances aside, a birth center may give you the low-tech birth experience you want—without resorting to a home birth. In general, women who deliver in birth centers tend to have fewer C-sections and are subject to fewer medical procedures, such as electronic fetal monitoring, forceps, and episiotomies. (Of course, this type of experience works best for low-risk, uncomplicated pregnancies.)

To find a birth center staffed by a certified nurse-midwife and accredited by the Commission for the Accredition of Freestanding Birth Centers (not all are), write to the National Association of Childbearing Centers: 3123 Gottschall Road, Perkiomenville, PA 18074; 215-234-8068. (Include a $1 processing fee.) Not all birth centers are licensed. Twenty-eight states, including New York, Georgia, and Massachusetts, have strict licensing requirements; the remaining states do not. To find out about licensing requirements in your state, contact your state health department.

Visit a birth center in person—well before the big day—and find out the following:

- What type of prenatal, childbirth, and postpartum care do you provide?

- Does the birth center operate within a hospital?

- If not, which hospital is the center affiliated with?

- Is the bulk of the care provided by certified nurse-midwives?

- What kind of physician backup is available?

- What emergency and/or life-support equipment do you have on-site?

- What happens in case of an emergency?

- What types of situations would cause transfer to a hospital during labor and delivery?

- Can the father attend the birth? Other family members, too?

- After birth, how long do the baby and mother stay at the birth center?
- What type of care is provided for the baby?

A *home birth* is the cheapest birth alternative. Often you pay just the midwife's professional fee. Home births have enjoyed something of a revival in recent years. But, although many prospective parents want a home*like* birth setting nowadays, very few opt to go with the real thing. How come? It can be risky. Should something go wrong—you need an emergency C-section or the baby needs to be resuscitated—that equipment isn't close at hand. And with even five or ten minutes to get you to the hospital it may be too late. What's more, it's difficult to find a licensed or certified practitioner who will come to your home. Most doctors feel it is dangerous, backward, and old-fashioned. And many certified nurse-midwives are restricted by state law from attending a home birth. Lay midwives are often your best, and only, alternative.

Still, many women want to give birth surrounded by family and friends and all the comforts of home. Others who live in rural areas far from a hospital or clinic may have no other choice. For more information about safe home births, contact the National Association of Parents and Professionals for Safe Alternatives in Childbirth: Route 1, Box 646, Marble Hill, MO 63763; 314-238-2010.

WHAT TO EXPECT FROM YOUR MEDICAL INSURANCE

Most couples depend on their health insurance to cover their doctor and hospital bills. In many cases, your medical coverage will pick up most but not all of the tab. Health insurance companies usually don't cover every medical treatment. They often set limits on how much they'll reimburse you for a certain procedure although your doctor may charge more. And they'll ask you to fork over an annual deductible before reimbursing you for any bills. After that, you'll probably be required to pay a small percentage of the bill, up to a predetermined amount.

All of these variables depend on the type of plan you have. There are three basic types: A traditional *fee-for-service plan* lets you pick your own doctor. A *preferred provider plan* allows you to see any of the doctors who participate in the plan's provider network (often, these plans will let you use a doctor outside the network, but you'll pay a bigger chunk of the bill). And a *health maintenance organization* (HMO) restricts coverage to doctors who are part of the group.

With each of these plans, you'll probably have a *deductible* that can range from $100 to $2,000 or more. If you have a policy with a $200 deductible, for example, you must pay $200 worth of your medical bills each year before your insurance kicks in.

Most policies have an individual deductible as well as a family deductible, meaning that once you reach the family deductible, your insurer will start reimbursing you for bills—even if each individual member hasn't met the deductible. Let's say your individual deductible is $200, but your family deductible is $500. You've just given birth to twin girls. Assuming you've incurred no other medical expenses this year, you'd have to pay the first $200 of your hospital bill, the first $200 of one daughter's hospital bill, but just the first $100 of your other daughter's hospital bill. Your insurance would then kick in because you'd met the family deductible of $500.

After you've met your deductible requirements, the insurer will start paying your bills. You're not off the hook yet, though. You'll probably still have to fork over some portion of each bill, called the *copayment*. With both a fee-for-service plan and a preferred provider plan, you'll pay a certain percentage—often 20% of the allowable bill. With an HMO, however, you'll pay a set amount instead—ranging from $5 to $15 per bill. Under all three plans, you'll be required to make copayments until you reach a certain "out-of-pocket maximum," at which point the insurer will pay 100% of your medical bills.

Unfortunately, you probably won't get one neat little bill that itemizes your maternity care. The hospital or birth center itself will send you a series of bills depending on the services rendered. If you had an epidural, for instance, you'll get a bill from the anesthesiologist. You'll get another bill for your hospital stay. Another for the baby's hospital stay. And probably still another for the pediatrician who checked him out. Want Junior to be circumsized? That's another bill.

Some hospitals and birth centers will bill the insurance company directly. That will save you some paperwork. (Otherwise, you'll have to file the claim yourself.) Once they receive payment, the hospital will then bill you for whatever the insurance company did not pay. That amount will vary, depending on your deductible and copayments.

Generally, your insurer will pay for "reasonable and customary" charges, an amount the insurance company deems fair payment for service. Often, it can fall far short of the actual bill. If an anesthesiologist charges $5,000 for a spinal but your insurance company thinks that $3,500 is the reasonable and customary charge for that particular medical service, you'll be expected to foot the difference ($1,500 in this case).

In some cases, your insurer will deny a claim completely. That means they won't pay a dime because of noncoverage. Perhaps your insurance doesn't cover such procedures.

You'll have to check your plan's handbook. Some private insurance companies don't cover a midwife's services, for instance. Or, perhaps your insurance covers such procedures only under certain conditions. Many insurers don't cover amniocentesis, for example, if you're under 35 years of age. Even if you meet the age limit, some insurers won't pay unless your doctor writes a note saying the test was a "medical necessity." (See Figure 1.3.)

You and your spouse may have separate insurers. You can submit your claims to both. One insurer may pay what another doesn't. Generally, you should submit the claim to the mother's insurer first. (That's your "primary" insurer, in this case.) After the mother's insurance company has paid its share, send it to the father's company (the "secondary" insurer) to pick up the balance.

If neither insurance company covers such a fee (and you feel it's legitimate) or both insurance companies reimburse for reasonable and customary charges that you think are too low, you can fight it.

Start by contacting the insurer. Explain your situation, and ask for an explanation. (Be sure to note the date, time, and person you spoke with.) Follow up with a letter. The insurer will probably write back in a few weeks saying that this is its policy and, sorry, there's nothing it can do about it. You can then pay the bill, or, if you feel you really have a case, complain to your State Insurance Department. That will involve another round of letters. (Be sure to include copies of your previous correspondence with the insurance company.) You still may not win your case, but the insurance department will make sure that you get a thorough answer from your insurance company.

Still not satisfied? Take the matter to a lawyer who specializes in insurance matters. Or work out a deal with the doctor. Here's what I did: After my son was born prematurely,

FIGURE 1.3   WHAT'S COVERED?

As soon as you find out that you're pregnant—or before, if you're very organized—get the details about maternity benefits from your insurance company. Confirm your individual and family deductibles, your copayments, and your out-of-pocket maximums. Find out if you have to advise your insurer of the impending birth ahead of time. Nowadays, many insurers won't cover a hospital stay unless contacted within 48 hours of admission. Some good questions to ask include:

Prenatal Care

How many doctor visits are covered? (Visits are usually more frequent as a pregnancy advances.)

Are the services of a midwife covered? Does the midwife have to be certified?

Which tests are covered? (Ask about amniocentesis. Many policies don't cover this.)

Sonograms? How many?

Prescriptions? What about vitamins?

Labor and Delivery Care

Is use of an epidural or some other anesthesia covered?

A cesarean section?

How many days can I stay in the hospital? How many days in the event of a C-section?

Is delivery in a birth center covered? (Some insurers will pay 100% of birth center delivery costs but just 80% of hospital delivery costs.)

Is delivery at home covered?

Care of the Baby

For how long?

Are visits from my pediatrician covered?

Which tests?

Procedures such as circumcision?

Intensive care?

he had to stay in intensive care for two weeks. He was assigned a pediatric neonatal specialist who was on the hospital staff. A bill for $4,300 arrived, and my insurer would
allow just $2,500 as a "reasonable fee" for such care. Being
a frugal money manager, I wasn't about to pay the $1800
difference. So I wrote letter after letter to the insurance
company and my State Insurance Department. Nothing
worked. Finally, after several dunning notices from my
doctor, I called his office to explain the situation. And lo
and behold, he split the difference with me. The man actually lowered his bill! I wrote him a check for $900 that very
afternoon.

IF YOU DON'T HAVE INSURANCE

An estimated 36 million Americans don't have health insurance. Some people simply can't afford to buy coverage.
Others are denied coverage outright because of a history
of illness, or their preexisting condition is excluded from
coverage.

If you can't afford health insurance, your state health department may be able to refer you to a free or low-cost clinic
in your area. If you've been laid off from a job or your hours
have been cut back so that you're no longer eligible for insurance, COBRA (Consolidated Omnibus Budget Reconcil-
iation Act) gives you the right to keep your benefits in your
employer's group health plan for up to 18 months. If you
become disabled and can't work anymore, you have the
same right for up to 29 months. And if you are divorced,
legally separated, or your insured spouse dies, you have the
right to continue participating in the company plan for up
to 36 months. Of course, your employer won't give you this
coverage for free. Expect to pay the full premium yourself—
plus a 2% administration charge. A company's group rate is
cheaper than buying an individual policy, but it may still be
expensive.

If you can afford to buy insurance—but don't have it because you're between jobs or you're not eligible for health coverage at your job—you can frequently buy coverage through professional organizations. Members of the National Association of Female Executives, for example, can buy individual and family coverage. It's not cheap, but it's less costly than footing the maternity bill yourself.

When buying a new policy, keep in mind that pregnancy is considered a preexisting condition. Be sure to buy the policy *before* you get pregnant. If you buy a policy after you've already conceived, none of your maternity care will be covered. (The baby's hospital and doctor bills will be covered, however.)

QUESTIONS AND ANSWERS

Q. Will my insurance company pay for a midwife?

A. Most private health insurers, as well as Medicaid and Medicare, will reimburse you for a nurse-midwife's services. It generally doesn't matter whether the birth occurs at home, in a birth center, or at a hospital. A sticky point that should be addressed ahead of time: What happens if complications arise and an obstetrician is called in at the last minute to perform a cesarean section? Some insurance companies won't pay for both a doctor *and* a certified nurse-midwife.

Q. I requested a private room during my hospital stay, but was given a semiprivate room instead. Now I'm being billed for a private room. What recourse do I have?

A. It's not surprising to find errors in your hospital bill. Hospitals bill patients for services and supplies when they're ordered—not when they're actually delivered. Perhaps the hospital intended to give you a private room but there wasn't one available when you needed it. You can correct the error by calling the hospital. If the problem isn't immediately resolved (it should be), follow up with a written letter to the hospital administrator.

Q. My husband and I have separate medical insurance policies through our jobs. Can we both claim my maternity expenses?

A. Yes, but you can't make money on the deal. Although you may be able to get all of your medical costs covered by your insurance, you won't be reimbursed for more than 100% of the bill. Here's how it works: You should first submit your claim to your primary insurer. (When you both have plans, the wife's plan is usually primary for her, the husband's plan is primary for him.) After you have collected from your primary insurer, you can then file the remaining expenses—including documentation of what the primary insurer has already paid—with your secondary insurer. Often, that policy will pick up whatever expenses the first policy did not.

Q. When can I add my newborn to my health insurance policy?

A. As soon as the baby is born, or legally adopted. He or she should be covered automatically if you have a family policy. But check with your insurer beforehand to make sure.

Q. Is midwifery legal in all states?

A. Yes. Certified nurse-midwives (but not lay midwives) are legally able to assist in low-risk, uncomplicated births in all 50 states and the District of Columbia. What else can a nurse-midwife do? That depends on the state. In Alabama, for instance, nurse-midwives can't deliver a breech baby or multiple pregnancies, or use forceps. In Idaho, nurse-midwives can administer pitocin (a drug frequently given to hasten labor). And, in all but a few states, certified nurse-midwives can write prescriptions. For more information on your state's laws, contact your state licensing board.

FOR MORE INFO

Check out the *National Association of Childbearing Centers'* Web site (www.birthcenters.org) for some general information on childbearing centers.

Contact *Informed Homebirth/Informed Birth & Parenting* if you're thinking about a home birth: Box 3675, Ann Arbor, MI; 313-662-6857.

The *People's Medical Society*, a consumer health care group, publishes a newsletter and a variety of consumer health books such as *So You're Going to Be a Mother* and *The Savvy Medical Consumer*. Contact them at: 462 Walnut Street, Lower Level, Allentown, PA 18102; 800-624-8773.

The *American Board of Medical Specialties* will send you its booklet, "Which Medical Specialist for You?" when you write to them (and include a $1.50 fee): 1007 Church Street, Suite 404, Evanston, IL 60201-5913.

CHAPTER TWO

———— $ ————

If You Have Difficulty Conceiving

Conceiving a child isn't always easy. Sometimes it's downright impossible. That may mean you'll have to seek alternative strategies for bringing a baby into your lives. Unfortunately, the diagnosis and treatment of infertility, as well as the pursuit of adoption, are expensive ventures. Testing, frequent office visits, medication, and assisted reproductive technology (ART) treatment can quickly consume thousands of dollars. In vitro fertilization, for instance, costs about $10,000 and often doesn't work the first time around. Domestic or international adoption proceedings are just as costly.

To finance the undertaking of infertility therapy, which often lasts several years or longer, many people rely on medical insurance coverage. But insurance doesn't completely cover infertility treatments. In many cases, insurance doesn't cover them at all. If your insurer doesn't cover these procedures—or if you don't have medical coverage—you'll have to draw from your savings, obtain an equity loan against your house, get a second job, or borrow from friends and relatives. Couples determined to conceive or adopt a child will often, understandably, deplete every last financial resource, and put themselves severely in debt. But, bear in mind that this is just one cost in raising a child. You'll still need plenty of money in the coming years for karate lessons, Happy Meals at McDonald's, and college tuition.

THE INFERTILITY PROBLEM

Infertility affects 1 out of every 12 couples in the United States. That means 4.9 million people are unable to conceive a baby after a year of trying (the medical definition of infertility), or are unable to bring a pregnancy to term. What's wrong? Some men can't produce enough sperm or sperm strong enough to penetrate the egg. Some woman don't ovulate regularly, have blocked fallopian tubes, or suffer from endometriosis. Sometimes the problem lies with both partners; sometimes there is no explanation. And, increasingly, the problem is that couples delay childbearing until they're in their mid-30s or early 40s when the woman can get pregnant only with great difficulty, if at all.

Your first step in the infertility cycle is to determine why you can't get pregnant. That will cost you, of course. A full diagnostic workup, which includes both partners, multiple office visits, and often a day in the hospital, costs $1,500 to $3,000, on average. (See Figure 2.1 for tests that may be required.) Fortunately, most insurance plans cover this diagnostic work. During this evaluation phase, a couple may occasionally get pregnant without any specific treatment. But, generally, most couples take these early tests to determine the next course of action: Which fertility treatment is appropriate?

FIGURE 2.1   THE DIAGNOSIS OF INFERTILITY

HIS	HERS
Semen analysis	Monitoring of basal body temperature
Postcoital test	Postcoital test
Sperm penetration assay	Hysterosalpingogram
Sperm antibody test	Hysteroscopy
Serum antibody test	Endometrial biopsy
Blood hormone analysis	Blood hormone analysis
Vasogram	Ultrasound
Testicular biopsy	Cervical antibody test
	Serum antibody test
	Mycomplasma and chlamydia cultures
	Laparoscopy

After the cause(s) of infertility have been identified, treatment options may include one or more of the following procedures:

Female

Drug therapy to induce ovulation

Antibiotic therapy

Microsurgery to repair fallopian tubes

Laparoscopic surgery

Hysteroscopic surgery

Fibroid surgery

Surgery to treat endometriosis

Therapy for immunologic infertility

Male

Antibiotic therapy

Varicocele surgery

FIGURE 2.1 (CONTINUED)

Male (Continued)
Microsurgery to assist sperm flow
Hormonal therapy
Therapy for immunologic infertility
Couple
Husband or donor insemination
Intrauterine insemination

Assisted reproductive technologies:
  In vitro fertilization
  Gamete intrafallopian transfer
  Zygote intrafallopian transfer

Source: Reprinted with permission by Resolve, from "Infertility and National Health Care Reform: A Briefing Paper." Copyright © 1992.

You have a handful of choices these days. Some are much costlier than others. (See Figure 2.2.) Low-tech options such as drug therapy and artificial insemination are considerably cheaper and require far less time and effort than high-tech alternatives such as in vitro fertilization and zygote intrafallopian transfer. None guarantee success. And many women do not become pregnant after the first attempt. Generally, the older you are, the more attempts you're likely to need. According to Resolve Inc., the infertility support group, at least 50% of those who complete an infertility evaluation will respond to treatment with a successful pregnancy.

Artificial insemination. More than 11,000 doctors offer artificial insemination as a treatment for infertility. Insemination using sperm from the husband is the most popular type. Other couples use a donor's sperm, however. Sperm banks, which supply anonymous sperm, are loosely regu-

FIGURE 2.2   AT A GLANCE: THE COST OF INFERTILITY

Here are some average costs for the more common procedures used to treat infertility:

PROCEDURE	CHARGES
Drug therapy to induce ovulation	$60–$700
Intrauterine insemination	$300
In vitro fertilization (IVF)	$10,000
Gamete intrafallopian transfer (GIFT)	$13,000

lated, so pick one that's affiliated with the American Association of Tissue Banks (1350 Beverly Road, McLean, VA 22101; 703-827-9582), or one that follows the guidelines of the American Society for Reproductive Medicine.

In vitro fertilization (IVF). Since 1978, when Louise Brown was born in England, about 33,000 IVF babies have been born in the United States. The procedure is legal, has become standard medical practice, and is offered at over 200 clinics throughout the country.

Here's how it works: A woman is given a drug to stimulate the development of several eggs simultaneously. (Normally one egg develops each month.) When the eggs are mature, they are removed from the woman with a thin needle, guided by ultrasound or the surgical procedure laparoscopy. The five to seven eggs generally retrieved are then placed in a glass dish (in vitro means "in glass") and allowed to mature further for several hours. Afterward, they're mixed with a man's sperm, and, if fertilization occurs, two or three of the embryos (as they're now called) are transferred to the woman's uterus. The rest are frozen and stored for later use, if necessary.

The IVF procedure is generally considered a last-ditch

effort to be used only after all other conventional infertility therapies have failed. It's quite expensive: some $8,000 to $10,000 per procedure or attempt. After the transfer, the woman has to stay in bed for a few days and, in some cases, undergo some follow-up tests. Sometimes the procedure works the first time around. Other cases may require two or more cycles of treatment. Generally, it's recommended that you attempt up to six cycles of IVF (if you can afford it) prior to age 40; just four cycles after age 40.

Gamete intrafallopian transfer (GIFT). The GIFT procedure is an offshoot of in vitro fertilization. A woman's eggs and a man's sperm are mixed together and placed immediately in a woman's fallopian tubes. Fertilization is then supposed to take place naturally. Some documentation concludes that GIFT yields a higher pregnancy rate than IVF, especially in women over 40.

Zygote intrafallopian transfer (ZIFT). An even newer procedure commonly known as ZIFT works much like GIFT. In this case, however, the eggs are fertilized in a laboratory dish and then inserted into the woman's fallopian tubes. According to the most recent statistics, ZIFT has a higher live birthrate (29.1%) than both GIFT (28.5%) and IVF (21.1%).

Surrogate motherhood. MaryBeth Whitehead made headlines with this infertility option back in the 1980s when she reneged on her contract with the Sterns and tried to keep "Baby M," the child she bore them as a surrogate mother. Today, a typical surrogate motherhood arrangement involves an infertile couple wealthy enough to afford the high costs, up to $35,000. Generally, $12,000 to $16,000 of that amount is paid to the surrogate for bearing a child whom the couple will then adopt; the balance covers medical costs and legal fees charged by the surrogacy center that acts as intermediary.

Typically, a surrogate mother responds to an ad placed by a surrogacy center. The surrogate is then artificially inseminated (usually with the adopting male parent's sperm), carries the baby to term, and turns it over to the couple for adoption. (In some cases, a surrogate is implanted with both sperm and the egg. Her uterus is used merely to carry the couple's biological child to term.) The problem occurs, of course, when the surrogate changes her mind and wants to keep the baby. A costly and emotionally wrenching custody battle can ensue, as in the now-famous Baby M case.

FINANCING ASSISTED REPRODUCTION

Don't count on your medical coverage to pick up the tab. Many insurance companies refuse to pay for in vitro fertilization and other types of assisted reproductive technology (ART). Others pay for a very limited amount. Infertility isn't considered, by some insurers, to be a bona fide medical problem in the same way that an injury or an illness such as cancer is. Others consider many of these procedures to be experimental. And still others cite the low success rate of some of the procedures, which, they say, argues against coverage.

The tide may finally be changing. Due to efforts by consumer groups like Resolve, 10 states—Arkansas, California, Connecticut, Hawaii, Illinois, Maryland, Massachusetts, New York, Rhode Island, and Texas—now require insurance companies to cover infertility treatments, including in vitro fertilization. How much coverage is actually provided under these new laws varies by state. Some states require insurers to give 100% coverage; others merely require insurers to offer coverage, which the employer has the option to purchase.

A handful of other states offer some laws or regulations regarding infertility, too. In Delaware, state employees are covered for in vitro fertilization and other assisted reproductive techniques. And in Ohio, West Virginia, and Montana, health maintenance organizations (HMOs) must provide infertility services.

To get the most for your money—and to lessen the chances of being bankrupted by one infertility treatment after another—get as much information on the subject as you can beforehand. Investigate the cause of your infertility (once you learn what it is) and what can be done. Find out about alternative treatments, the risks and costs involved, and the likelihood of success.

- Start by talking it over with your physician. What tests and procedures will be used? How much will they cost? (Trouble is, it's often tough to tell how much the final bill will actually be. One simple procedure may do the trick. Or you may need five in vitro attempts. Probably, the most you can hope for is a rough price estimate.)

- Ask what arrangements can be made for payments. Must you pay up front and wait to be reimbursed, or will the doctor send your bills to the insurance carrier first?

- Assume nothing in terms of your insurance coverage. Get a copy of your insurance policy and check it over carefully for limitations and exclusions. Even in states that mandate coverage, certain restrictions may apply. In Illinois, for instance, small businesses with fewer than 25 employees do not have to comply with the state's infertility statute. If your policy does not specify how infertility claims are treated, contact your company benefits manager or the insurance company itself.

- Find out if your insurance plan has dollar limits or caps in place. At least one state, Arkansas, has set a lifetime cap of $15,000 on infertility treatments.

- Take advantage of the federal income tax deduction for medical expenses by grouping all infertility tests and treatments in a single year, if possible. Certain exclusions and requirements apply, of course.

- Set a time limit on treatment. A tough call, certainly, but tests, treatments, and their subsequent bills can go on forever. Too often, infertile couples will push themselves beyond their financial (and emotional) resources.

- Check out the location of the infertility clinic or center. Traveling to and from a distant medical center could add significantly to your out-of-pocket expenses, absenteeism from work, and overall level of stress.

WHERE TO SHOP FOR SERVICES

Let's assume that you and your spouse have been trying to conceive a child for at least a year (or six months, if you're over age 35). You haven't been successful. Initially, many women will seek help from their obstetrician/gynecologist, who can usually perform most of the tests needed for a preliminary fertility workup. Should you then discover that you require more advanced treatment and/or testing, though, you'll need a specialist.

Some ob/gyns are trained in fertility issues, too, but you'll probably need to find someone who is a "fertility specialist." Look for a physician who is board-certified or board-eligible in reproductive endocrinology. All licensed physicians, remember, have completed four years of medical school and passed board-approved exams. After a year of internship, some choose a specialty such as obstetrics and gynecology. A fertility specialist, however, will have some three years' *additional* education, training, and experience in the diagnosis and treatment of all aspects of female infertility. However, this specialist doesn't treat men. Most male patients are referred to an andrologist; that's a urologist who specializes in male reproductive problems.

A fertility specialist shouldn't be carrying a heavy obstetrical caseload, or you'll never get the attention that you need. Find out whether he or she specializes in a certain kind of treatment. And make sure to ask about success rate. You want to know how many patients actually take a baby home as opposed to pregnancies conceived. Some doctors (and clinics) inflate their success rate by counting *all* conceptions as successes, even those that end in miscarriage or otherwise fail.

You may decide to use a fertility clinic rather than just a private physician. To get the most for your time and money, you'll want to know about the doctors: How many will be involved in your care? What are their backgrounds? Are they trained in reproductive endocrinology? Do they offer counseling? Find out how long the clinic has been in business, and what its success rate is for the particular infertility problem you have. Ask if there's a waiting list and a payment schedule. Do they accept insurance payments? Unfortunately, most infertility clinics are still unregulated, so there is little consumer protection offered by state and federal government. You must be your own watchdog.

One place you'll want to check: the Society for Assisted Reproductive Technology (SART). This special interest group run by the American Society for Reproductive Medicine collects data on pregnancy rates from the clinics that report to them. The clinics undergo an accreditation process and possible on-site evaluation. For a copy of the SART report giving statistics on specific clinics, call 205-978-5000.

ADOPTION: THE OTHER OPTION

You want a baby with your spouse's eyes. Your nose. Your favorite aunt's smile. For many infertile couples who are desperate to have a child genetically related to at least one of the parents, adoption isn't an easy option to consider. Nor is it easy—or cheap—to find a suitable baby, should you ultimately decide to adopt. The pool of adoptable babies is shrinking, largely because of more effective birth control use, legalized abortion, and the growing number of single women who keep and raise their babies.

The National Council for Adoption estimates that two million couples compete to adopt the 52,000 babies who are placed for adoption in the United States every year. If you want a healthy Caucasian infant, the wait could be eight years, the cost $25,000 or more. Couples willing to adopt a nonwhite baby, an older child, several siblings, or a handicapped youngster, however, will likely get a child much faster and pay far less. Whatever type of child you decide to welcome into your family, you can't do it alone. Baby selling is illegal in every state, so you must adopt a child through an intermediary—either an adoption agency or a lawyer who specializes in adoption.

TRADITIONAL AGENCY ADOPTION

Adoption agencies are licensed, state-regulated private or public organizations that coordinate the adoption process between birth parents who wish to give up their child (or whose children are removed from their homes by the state) and couples or individuals seeking to adopt a child.

The wait is generally long, up to eight years. But the risk of a biological parent changing his or her mind is minimal: In most cases, the birth parents have already relinquished their rights and placed the child in the agency's care. Before you can add your name to the list, an agency must deem that you and your spouse will make suitable parents. Although agencies are more open to various lifestyles than they used to be—single parents, for instance, now frequently adopt children, whereas in the past they seldom did—you still must meet certain criteria. Do you have enough money to provide for a child? (Forget it if you're on welfare or unemployed.) Do you have a terminal illness, or is your marriage on the rocks? (Being already divorced won't disqualify you, but an adoption agency won't want to place a child in a home that's liable to break up soon.) Are you over age 40? (This won't nix your application outright but it may make you less than an ideal candidate.) These questions and more are asked during the "home study" process. At some point, an adoption worker will visit your home, not to check up on your housecleaning skills, but, rather, to see that you can provide a safe and nurturing environment for a child.

Fees range from a few hundred dollars to about eight thousand dollars, depending on whether the organization is a nonprofit agency or a for-profit service. For-profit agencies are costlier than nonprofits because they're rarely subsidized by the state. A national agency will generally charge more than a local one. Costs for doctors, lawyers, care of the birth mother, and the agency's overhead (including the adoption worker's salary) are factored into that fee. Sliding-scale fees based on your income do exist, and some employers and insurance companies may cover all or part of the adoption expense.

INTERNATIONAL ADOPTION

If you can cope with a child of a different race or culture, you might consider an international adoption. More infants are orphaned or abandoned in foreign countries than in the United States, so the adoptable baby pool is bigger. But that doesn't mean it's easier. Or cheaper.

Laws differ from country to country, and they change frequently, depending on the particular situation at that moment. One year, Korean babies are flying across the border into American arms; 10 months later, the doors might be closed to Yanks. (See Figure 2.3.) In many cases, you'll learn little about the birth family's health and background. Mothers in poverty-stricken or war-torn countries probably had no prenatal care. And you'll have to fill out reams of paperwork to satisfy your own state's adoption requirements as well as the requirements of the Immigration and

FIGURE 2.3 A MELTING POT OF ADOPTEES

COUNTRY	NUMBER OF CHILDREN ADOPTED BY U.S. COUPLES	
	1990	1996
All countries	7,093	11,340
Russian Federation	0	2,454
Mainland China	29	3,333
Vietnam	0	354
Honduras	197	28
Korea	2,620	1,516
Philippines	421	229

Source: Reprinted with permission from the National Council for Adoption, 1930 17th Street, NW, Washington, DC 20009; 202-328-1200.

Naturalization Service (INS), the foreign country you're adopting from, and the adoption agency.

Like domestic adoptions, you can adopt internationally through an agency or privately. If you decide to go the private route, you'll still need a consultant agency here in the States to act as a liaison between your own country and the child's country. You may also want to hire an immigration attorney. The cost varies from country to country, mainly because of differences in what an international agency charges and if you choose to hire a liaison agency and an attorney. Plus, you'll have other expenses you might not incur with a domestic adoption. Generally, you have to go to the country to pick up the child, so expect to pay airfare for yourself. The process may require you to stay in the country for a few weeks. (See Figure 2.4.) That means you'll have to either plan your vacation around the adoption, or figure in

FIGURE 2.4 THE NECESSARY DATA

Whether you're traveling overseas to adopt a child or driving down to Florida to meet the birth mother, you'll need some documentation to move the adoption proceedings along. In most cases you will need to supply the following:

Birth certificates for each adoptive parent.

Marriage license.

Notarized current financial statement.

Previous year's income tax return.

Employer letters verifying your position and salary.

Medical records or exam for each adoptive parent.

Approved home study by licensed agency.

Passports for each adoptive parent (if it's an international adoption).

Letters of reference.

a brief leave of absence without pay. Don't forget to include the cost of eating meals out, using taxis or public transportation, and staying at a hotel. On average, an international adoption will cost you some $3,000 to $5,000 more than a domestic adoption.

SPECIAL NEEDS CHILDREN

While there's a scarcity of healthy Caucasian infants available for adoption, you'll find an abundance of children of all races—generally over the age of six—waiting for a home. Trouble is, many of them have learning disabilities or suffer from mental retardation or other emotional or physical handicaps. You can often adopt these kids within a short period of time because they're already available, and not in great demand. (Newborns born with the HIV virus or a crack dependency fall into this category, too.) You'll still have to undergo the home study process. Afterward, you'll work with the agency to select a child who is right for you, often by looking through what's known as the blue books. (These files include a photograph and brief family history of each child.) Agencies now frequently hold get-togethers, which give parents and kids the opportunity to meet in a relaxed setting.

The cost of such an adoption is usually minimal because it is subsidized by the state. Often, medical and counseling services are subsidized, too, and, depending on the type of care the child needs, you may even be able to get state and federal monies to fund the child's education at a special school.

LEGAL RISK ADOPTION

Like the special needs group, this adoption class is available, and often for no cost (the cost is subsidized by the state). But this type of adoption doesn't come without its problems. Often these kids come from troubled homes, where they may have been physically or psychologically abused. The biggest drawback, however, is that these children are not yet legally free for adoption, and they may never be. The birth parents may not want to surrender their rights to their child, but, for various reasons, have placed the child in foster care for the time being. Or, a legal battle could be pending that is challenging the validity of one parent's adoption surrender or a court order that terminated a parent's rights.

PRIVATE ADOPTION

In recent years, more and more couples have opted for an independent adoption, dealing directly with the birth mother through an intermediary—a lawyer, doctor, or adoption facilitator—rather than working with an adoption agency. Why? Fewer Caucasian babies are available through adoption agencies. Plus, you can bypass the stream of red tape and strict requirements typically imposed by agencies. (An agency will become involved only if your state requires a home study.)

All this will cost you more, in most cases. But isn't it illegal to sell a baby? Yes. What you pay for, technically, is the mother's medical care (and, in some states, her living expenses) and the intermediary's fee. Neither party (but especially not the birth mother) should be making a profit on the deal. Both fees, which together can reach $15,000 or so, should be set at the outset.

You're responsible for prenatal and neonatal medical expenses for both mom and baby. Most doctors and hospitals can estimate those costs in advance. But, if complications occur, those medical expenses can quickly escalate. Let's say that the birth mother delivers by cesarean section. That procedure carries higher doctor's fees and calls for a longer stay in the hospital. Let's further say that the baby is born several weeks premature. Just a 10-day stay in a neonatal intensive care unit will run you more than $4,000. In most cases, any medical insurance that an adoptive couple carry cannot be applied toward the birth mother's medical bills, but some of these expenses may be tax-deductible. (Check with your accountant.) A birth mother may have her own medical coverage, of course, or she may be eligible for Medicare or Medicaid.

A further wrinkle? If the birth mother changes her mind, you can't get your money back. You can't sue her for monies already paid, unless you can prove that she never intended to give the child up for adoption, or that she accepted money from you and from other families at the same time for the adoption of the same child.

Usually, the birth mother is found during the later stages of pregnancy, and, increasingly, she and the adoptive parents can meet. No matter how friendly the adoption seems, it is still a smart idea for adoptive parents to work with an intermediary. A family law practitioner who specializes in adoption is a popular, and excellent, choice to perform the necessary legal steps. It's crucial to have someone on your side who can negotiate a clear, contractual agreement with the birth mother that will not only outline the costs involved but that will prevent legal battles over the child in the future.

Some attorneys may even help you search for a baby. At the very least, a good lawyer will provide legal advice about adoption laws in your state (and the birth mother's state, if she lives elsewhere) and perform the required paperwork. Some may charge an hourly rate, $175 to $300 per hour. Others charge a flat fee ranging from $3,000 to $4,000. Under no circumstances should you be asked to pay an enormous sum for the child—a fee of say, $20,000, over and above all other expenses discussed. Some agencies that claim to be independent adoption facilitators may ask for an up-front nonrefundable fee.

Private adoption isn't legal in every state, but an "identified adoption" generally is. In cases like this, the couple identifies a baby that they want to adopt; an agency then comes in to counsel the birth mother, complete the couple's home study, and process the adoption. You get a baby quicker than you would through a traditional adoption proceeding—but you still work with an agency.

BLACK MARKET ADOPTION

How can you tell that a private adoption is actually a black market (or illegal) adoption? The cost. If you're paying more than $30,000, all costs should be carefully scrutinized. (See Figure 2.5.) Be especially wary if a big chunk of that money is due up front. A second sign: Your intermediary operates from a post office box address.

FIGURE 2.5 AT A GLANCE: THE COST OF ADOPTION

TYPE OF ADOPTION	CHILDREN AVAILABLE	WAITING TIME	COST
Agencies (domestic)	All infants; older children, some with special needs	One to eight years	$400–$8,000
International	Infants and older children from mainland China and Russian Federation	One to two years	$3,500–$21,000
Private	Caucasian infants, primarily	Less than one year	$14,000–$16,000

QUESTIONS AND ANSWERS

Q. I'm adopting an infant next month. What can I expect from my employer? Will it pick up any of my adoption tab? Will I get a maternity leave?

A. If you have a generous boss, yes. Some companies, such as Pfizer and Procter & Gamble, foot a portion of their employees' adoption costs. Other companies extend the same maternity leave to adoptive mothers that they give to biological mothers. (For details about maternity leave, disability, and other workplace issues, see Chapter 4.) Unfortunately, that's not always the case. Some adoptive mothers must use personal leave or take time off without being paid. The employer's explanation? The birth mother needs time physically to recover, while the adoptive mother does not.

Q. At this point, my doctor says that our best chance of conceiving a child is through in vitro fertilization. We have enough cash saved to pay for the procedures but my husband is worried we won't be able to afford the results if we're successful. Don't most IVF moms have twins, or more? Isn't there a higher incidence of birth defects?

A. About 66% of all IVF babies are singletons, 28% are twins, and 6% are triplets or more, according to the American Society for Reproductive Medicine. Twins and triplets are generally more expensive than a single child, but there are strategies to keep those costs down (see Chapter 3 for more details). Also, IVF babies are no more likely to be born with birth defects than children who are conceived naturally.

Q. Is the infant that we just adopted covered by my medical insurance?

A. Yes, but not necessarily from the moment he or she is placed in your arms. Policies vary. Some insurance companies will cover your adopted child from day one, but they will not cover any preexisting conditions. Other insurers won't cover your child until the adoption has been finalized. Federal law, however, requires most employer-provided health plans to treat adoptive children the same as birth children; neither can be excluded from coverage for a preexisting condition as long as the child is added to the plan within 30 days of becoming eligible.

Q. I belong to an HMO. Are they less likely to cover in vitro fertilization than a prepaid insurance plan?

A. No. But they may have some restrictions. Some HMOs, for instance, will cover only in vitro clinics that have at least a three-year track record. Before signing up for any costly procedures, call your insurer first to find out what's covered.

Q. I'm interested in arranging a private adoption. Will I be responsible for all of the birth mother's expenses?

A. Most likely you'll be responsible for all the medical costs related to the pregnancy. That includes prenatal care, delivery, and hospital costs. In some cases, parents have been able to get the birth mother's medical expenses covered under their own health plans; in other instances, parents have had to foot the entire bill. In many cases the birth mother has medical insurance or is covered by Medicare or Medicaid so you'll be responsible for the portion that isn't covered by her insurance—namely, the deductible, the coinsurance, and any tests or other fees that are not covered. You may also be asked to cover other expenses such as dental care, the cost for food and/or housing, and even counseling. Some states allow these expenses to be paid by adoptive parents; others do not.

FOR MORE INFO

Resolve Inc. is a nationwide education and advocacy network for infertile couples. Call their help line (617-623-0744) with questions about infertility or adoption. There are 60 local chapters nationwide that provide support to infertile couples and offer a newsletter and fact sheets on infertility and alternatives. Contact Resolve at: 1310 Broadway, Somerville, MA 02144-1731. Their Web site address is www.resolve.org.

The *American Society for Reproductive Medicine* offers several thorough pamphlets such as "IVF & GIFT: A Guide to Assisted Reproductive Technologies" and "Infertility: An Overview; A Guide for Patients" for just one dollar apiece. Contact the society at: 1209 Montgomery Highway, Birmingham, AL 35216-2809; 205-978-5000.

Call the *American Academy of Adoption Attorneys,* a national association of attorneys who handle adoption cases, for a listing of their members: 202-832-2222.

The *North American Council on Adoptable Children* (NACAC) offers information on special needs adoption and maintains a list of parent support groups. Contact the council at: 970 Raymond Avenue, Suite 106, St. Paul, MN 55114; 612-644-3036.

Write or call the *National Council for Adoption* for its free info packet on how to pick an agency. The packet will include a list of some adoption agencies in your area. The council's *Adoption Fact Book* (1989) is an excellent source of information: 1930 17th Street NW, Washington, DC 20009; 202-328-1200.

Visit the Adoption Exchange on the Internet at www.adoptex.org.

CHAPTER THREE

$

Baby Gear

The possibilities are endless. Walk into any baby store around the country and you'll be amazed at the vast array of baby stuff that's available. Need a pacifier? You'll find not just one, but dozens, all in different shapes and sizes. Shopping for a car seat? You can choose from infant, full, or booster sizes, plus those that snap into matching strollers. Want some time-saving devices? Diaper Genies wrap dirty diapers up in compact, odor-free casings; bottle warmers heat formula to the perfect temperature in minutes; automatic swings can rock baby nonstop for days.

If you're a first-time parent, you'll probably be tempted to load up before the little shaver is born. You may find yourself buying one or more of everything and spending to the max, because nothing is too good for your child. But by the time you're ready to welcome baby number two or three, you'll probably lower your standards a bit. Not everything must be top of the line anymore, and you don't necessarily need every IQ builder or soothe-to-sleep gizmo on the market. Mostly, you've learned how fast babies grow. It's smarter to keep purchases down now, and spend more *later*, when it really counts.

So what do you need during pregnancy and the first year? A working wardrobe for expectant moms. A basic wardrobe for baby. And a few essentials for the tiny tot: namely, a place to sleep, eat, and play. In this chapter you'll also learn how much you can expect to spend on these essentials and where you can cut corners to save a few bucks.

WARDROBE FOR THE MOM-TO-BE

These duds aren't your mother's maternity clothes. Gone are the frilly smocks in pastel shades that made you look as though you had regressed to childhood yourself. Instead, you'll find a variety of comfortable, yet fashionable, garb: everything you need to take you from the office to the playground to a night out on the town.

But it'll cost you. Maternity clothes are pricier than regular-sized stuff and rarely go on sale, except if the store is trying to sell end-of-season merchandise. (I'm not sure who buys these sale items. By next summer, for instance, you won't need those maternity shorts you can scoop up for half-price now because you won't be pregnant anymore.) Small boutiques specialize in maternity fashions, but you can also find mom-to-be basics at the larger national department store chains like Sears and Kmart.

How much you need and how much you'll ultimately spend depend on your situation. If you're already a stay-at-home mom, you can make do with simple weekend-style clothing, plus some new bras (generally you can't fit into your old bras due to breast expansion) and underwear. (See Figure 3.1.) In fact, you don't even necessarily have to wear maternity clothes. Regular leggings in a larger size worn with an oversized shirt will work just fine, especially for the earlier

FIGURE 3.1   AT A GLANCE: THE COST
OF AT-HOME MATERNITY CLOTHES

ITEM	SUGGESTED QUANTITY	COST	HOW MANY YOU NEED	YOUR COST
Jeans/pants	4	$100		
Blouses	4	$80		
T-shirts	4	$60		
Bras	6	$90		
Underwear	6	$30		
Low-heeled casual shoes	1	$55		
Swimsuit	1	$70		
Casual dresses	2	$100		
Short coat	1	$150		
Sweater/sweatshirt	2	$60		
Suggested Total Cost		$795	Your Total Cost $	

months. Even at regular price, these items are cheaper than most maternity outfits. Some women save more by raiding their husbands' closets for T-shirts and sweatpants.

But if you're a corporate lawyer, you'll need maternity suits, dresses, or whatever you normally wear to the office, too. In this case, you probably have no choice but to outfit yourself with an entirely new wardrobe. (See Figure 3.2.) Before you go on a shopping spree, however, remember that you're going to wear these clothes for a relatively short period of time. And no matter how striking you think that black maternity jumpsuit is, you won't want to wear these clothes postpartum. There isn't a woman alive who can't wait to slip back into her regular jeans.

If this is your first baby (and you don't expect it to be your

FIGURE 3.2   AT A GLANCE: THE COST OF AT-WORK MATERNITY CLOTHES

ITEM	SUGGESTED QUANTITY	COST	HOW MANY YOU NEED	YOUR COST
Suits	4	$800		
Blouses to match suits	6	$150		
Dresses	4	$320		
Pantyhose	12	$60		
Low-heeled dress shoes	2	$140		
Full-length coat	1	$250		
Suggested Total Cost		$1,720	Your Total Cost $	

last), you may envision getting two terms out of these clothes. But that only works if you're pregnant during the same seasons. To get your money's worth, buy clothes in a few basic colors that you can easily mix and match. Pick fabrics like cotton that breathe. (During pregnancy your metabolism rises, making you feel warmer generally.) You can always layer clothing if you're chilly. Perhaps you can borrow some of your friends' outfits. Since you don't wear these clothes very long, they generally don't wear out. And buy as you "grow" rather than all at once. Despite what the saleswoman may say, you don't really know how you're going to look in your seventh month (some women carry high, low, big, or small) until you get closer to that point.

BABY'S FIRST WARDROBE

Your little guy or gal needs clothes, too. But before you buy up every bunting and bib in the layette department, arm yourself with a list of essentials and stick with it. Why? Once Junior arrives, the gifts will start pouring in. If they send clothes, most people tend to buy things that will fit the baby now or within the next several months. In addition, you'll probably be getting some hand-me-downs from relatives or friends; and, since newborns don't wear out their clothes, these items will probably look brand-new.

In all likelihood, you'll also be doing the baby's laundry a few times each week (sometimes daily), so you don't really need to buy that many clothes in the beginning. Should you find yourself running short, you can always fill in later on; this is a smarter tactic moneywise than being stuck with six seersucker sundresses that your daughter outgrew before she ever had a chance to wear them.

You must buy some things ahead of time, of course. Figure 3.3 outlines a basic wardrobe complete with prices. Bear in mind, however, the following tips when you go out shopping:

- *Know your sizes.* Baby clothes are sized by age: There are a 3-month size, a 6-month size, a 9-month size, and so on. Generally, clothes run small, so you should buy one size ahead. Most six-month-old babies, for instance, wear 9- or 12-month sizes. An exception: Clothing from babyGap runs true to size.

- *Keep the tags on.* You may have a larger-than-average baby and those newborn sizes won't cut it for more than a week or two. As long as the tags are still on the clothes or they're in their original packaging, you can probably exchange them for another size.

- *Bigger is better.* Babies grow very fast during their first year. For average-sized newborns, it's generally smarter to buy 3-month-size clothing instead of the "newborn" or "layette" size. Initially, you can just roll up the sleeves. Besides, the baggy look is always fashionable for babies.

- *Forgo the prepackaged layette.* Those colorfully-wrapped baskets are sure to include items you don't want or need. In-

FIGURE 3.3   AT A GLANCE: THE COST OF A LAYETTE

ITEM	SUGGESTED QUANTITY	COST	HOW MANY YOU NEED	YOUR COST
Undershirts	6	$19.50		
Stretchies	6	$54.00		
Nightgowns	4	$28.00		
Blanket sleepers	2	$20.00		
Booties/socks	3	$10.00		
Bibs	3	$7.50		
Sweaters	2	$30.00		
Hats	2	$11.00		
Bunting	1	$25.00		
Receiving blankets	4	$30.00		
Fitted sheets:				
For bassinet	3	$15.00		
For crib	3	$24.00		
Hooded towels	2	$18.00		
Washcloths	3	$6.00		
Cloth diapers*	12	$20.00		
Suggested Total Cost		$318.00	Your Total Cost $	

*To be used as burp cloths. For the cost of regular diapers, see "Bottoms Up" section.

stead, use a prepackaged layette as a guideline and individually pick the items you want. It'll cost less in the long run.

- *Keep it simple.* Babies spit up a lot and have to be changed frequently, so you'll want clothes that you can get on and off easily. Stretchies are the most useful in the early weeks, especially those that snap (rather than button) down the front. Fancy lace collars may look sweet but they'll probably scratch the baby and get in the way during feeding. If you buy overalls or sunsuits, make sure the bottoms open easily for changing so you don't have to take the whole outfit off.

SWINGS, STROLLERS, SEATS, AND OTHER NECESSITIES

Do you really need all of this stuff as soon as the baby arrives? Of course not. But some parents—especially those new to the game—want everything in place before Junior arrives on the scene, and they want it all to coordinate. The Winnie the Pooh comforter matches the Winnie the Pooh mobile, which matches the Winnie the Pooh nightlight, which matches. . . .

In truth, most parents buy several items that they need immediately, such as a car seat and a crib, and hope the bulk of the remaining items will be given as baby or shower gifts. (If you're superstitious about receiving a baby shower before the baby's actual arrival, suggest a "welcome to the world" party afterward instead.) You can always borrow a few things from friends or relatives. Just make sure that they meet current codes of safety. If the crib is a family heirloom manufactured 40 years ago, for instance, check to see that the bars are no more than $2\frac{3}{8}$ inches apart (considered safe by today's standards). Still missing some equipment? Hold off on buying items until you need them. You won't need a high chair or a baby seat for the bathtub, for instance, until your baby can sit up (about six months old). You may have more ready cash at that point, or better understand the features you need. At the very least, you won't have to store it for the next few months.

Prices and usage of all these items vary widely. A Peg Perego full-size stroller that's considered to be the best in its class costs some $350; an economy model costs just $75. Some people swear by infant swings; others never use them. A separate changing table is handy, but many folks—especially those living in a cramped apartment—just change the baby in the crib. And, for most new parents, a plain old rocking chair and walker aren't good enough anymore: These days, it seems you need a glider (with a matching footstool if you're a nursing mom) and an exersaucer, which lets your six-month-old jump up and down in place. As for diapers, I've had three babies but have yet to invest in one of those fancy diaper disposals. I just take the garbage out more frequently.

Figures 3.4 and 3.5 give a ballpark range of prices so you'll have some idea how to budget for these items. But in many cases, you're bound to find cheaper and/or pricier versions at stores in your area.

FIGURE 3.4   AT A GLANCE: THE COST OF BABY FURNISHINGS

ITEM	COST	DO YOU NEED IT?	YOUR COST
Bassinet	$50–$180		
Cradle	$150–$280		
Crib	$100–$550		
Crib set (includes bumper, sheet, dust ruffle, and comforter)	$40–$350		
Changing table	$50–$200		
Chest of drawers	$75–$650		
Glider	$200–$350		
Footstool	$40		
Estimated Total Cost	$705–$2,600	Your Total Cost	$

FIGURE 3.5 AT A GLANCE: THE COST OF BABY EQUIPMENT

ITEM	COST	DO YOU NEED IT?	YOUR COST
Swing	$65–$100		
Infant car seat	$55–$150		
Full-size car seat	$50–$170		
Full-size stroller	$75–$350		
Collapsible stroller	$25–$350		
Pram	$400–$700		
Exersaucer	$45–$85		
High chair	$48–$170		
Playpen	$60–$160		
Portable crib	$75–$125		
Bathtub	$10–$20		
Diaper pail/Diaper Genie	$15–$30		
Crib mobile	$18–$43		
Night light	$2–$20		
Monitor	$40		

Infant carrier:
  Front-carrier
  Back-carrier
	
	$20–$70
	$35–$90		

Infant seat	$30–$60		
Diaper bag	$13–$40		
Video monitor	$170		
Busy Box	$10–$25		
Pacifiers	$1–$4		
Baby Wipes warmer	$20–$25		
Bath seat	$10–$30		

FIGURE 3.5 (CONTINUED)

ITEM	COST	DO YOU NEED IT?	YOUR COST
Thermometer:			
Rectal	$4		
Ear	$50–$75		
Security gates	$25–$50		
Safety plugs for outlets	$1–$3		
Cassette player	$15–$50		
Soothing bedtime music	$5–$30		
Estimated Total Cost	$1,392–$3,239	Your Total Cost	$

BOTTOMS UP

In the first few months, babies basically eat, sleep, and use up one diaper after another. Simple activities for sure, but don't underestimate their cost. A year's worth of Pampers will run you about $650; a year's worth of formula, $840.

For the first four months, you'll need formula around the clock if you're not nursing; most pediatricians don't advise giving cereal or other solid food before this time. How much you spend on formula depends, believe it or not, on how much prep work you're willing to do. (See Figure 3.6.) A 32-ounce can of premixed, ready-to-pour Enfamil with iron, for example, costs $4.09, while a 13-ounce can of Enfamil concentrate that mixes with water to make 26 ounces costs just $2.99, and a 16-ounce can of Enfamil powder that mixes with water to make 118 ounces sells for $10.99. (That $840 estimate for the year that I used above assumes you're using the middle-priced concentrate formula.) In addition, you'll need bottles (either the traditional plastic ones or the disposable Playtex variety), nipples, a bottle brush, and possibly a sterilizer and a bottle warmer to keep at baby's bedside.

FIGURE 3.6 AT A GLANCE: THE COST OF FORMULA

ITEM	COST	WHAT YOU NEED	YOUR COST
Formula:			
Ready-to-use	$4.09		
Concentrate	$2.99		
Bottles:			
Plastic, reusable	$1.29		
Plastic holders	$4.00		
Disposable bottle liners (80 8-oz. size)	$5.00		
Nipples (two-pack)	$1–$3		
Bottle brush	$1.50–$5		
Sterilizer	$32–$50		
Bottle warmer	$10–$40		
Estimated Total Cost	$48.78–$111.09 Your Total Cost $		

Breast-feeding is cheaper, but not exactly free. (See Figure 3.7.) If you're going back to work or even just out for the evening, you'll need a breast pump. You can use one of those inexpensive hand pumps that the hospital often gives you for free, but this method is slow. A better bet: the Medela dual breast pump that you can either buy for about $225 or rent for $50 per month. You'll also need nursing bras (about $20 each) and nursing pads (about $5 for three dozen) to prevent leakage.

Once Junior turns four or five months, you can probably add cereal and some other solid food to his diet. You can chop, grind, or mush your own table food, of course, but most parents buy the jar variety. Small jars cost about 59 cents apiece, the larger size 69 cents. Over that first year, you'll buy, on average, 530 jars of carrots, applesauce, macaroni and beef dinner, and the like. That'll set you back at least $313.

**FIGURE 3.7   AT A GLANCE: THE COST
OF BREAST FEEDING**

ITEM	COST	WHAT YOU NEED	YOUR COST
Breast pump:			
Manual	$20–$35		
Electric/battery	$50–$70		
Dual electric	$225		
Bottles:			
Plastic, reusable	$1.29		
Plastic holders	$4.00		
Disposable bottle			
liners (80 8-oz. size)	$5.00		
Nipples (two-pack)	$1–$3		
Bottle brush	$1.50–$5		
Nursing bras (three)	$60.00		
Nursing pads (thirty-six)	$5.00		
Estimated Total Cost	$88.79–$307	Your Total Cost	$

What goes in must come out. When you're not feeding the little nipper during that first year, you'll most likely be changing his or her diaper. Expect to lay out about $55 per month for Pampers. If you're planning on using cloth diapers, expect to spend about $15 weekly for a diaper laundry service. Obviously, you could wash the diapers yourself and save some money, but it's questionable how much you'd actually gain. The cost of soap and water—plus the time and energy spent soaking, washing, and folding the diapers—makes the savings less dramatic. (See Figures 3.8 and 3.9.)

Which diapers should you use—cloth or disposable? The controversy is ongoing. Disposables are more convenient: They're easier to put on and take off and require no pins. They're more absorbent and, theoretically, less likely to cause diaper rash. But cloth-diaper advocates complain

FIGURE 3.8   AT A GLANCE: THE COST OF DISPOSABLE DIAPERS

ITEM	COST	WHAT YOU NEED	YOUR COST
Disposable diapers (one year's worth)	$650		
Diaper pail/Diaper Genie	$15–$30		
Estimated Total Cost	$680	Your Total Cost	$

FIGURE 3.9   AT A GLANCE: THE COST OF CLOTH DIAPERS

ITEM	COST	WHAT YOU NEED	YOUR COST
Diaper pail	$15		
Diaper service (pick up and delivery of 80 diapers—a week's supply)	$15		
Diaper covers (used instead of pins; need about four @ $7 each)	$28		
Estimated Total Cost	$58	Your Total Cost	$

that Pampers and their ilk are harmful to the environment because they're not biodegradable; they're filling up our already polluted planet. However, cloth diapers aren't purely "green" products either: You need a lot of detergent, water, and power to clean and sterilize cloth diapers. Another disadvantage is that because cloth diapers aren't as absorbent as disposables, the incidence of diaper rash increases.

Some parents use a combination of the two: disposables at night and for outings, the cloth variety at home. Your best bet is to ask friends and relatives what worked for them, and why. And then experiment. If your baby gets a rash frequently, for instance, switch to a different type of diaper (cloth to disposable or vice versa).

AND BABIES MAKE FIVE—OR MORE

Multiple births of three or more children are on the rise. According to the National Center for Health Statistics, there were 95.5 live births of three or more children per 100,000 births in 1992. In 1982, the number was 40.3; in 1972, just 27.8. What's causing this boomlet? The increased use of fertility drugs (about 28% of all in vitro fertilization babies are twins, 6% are triplets) and the advanced age of the mothers themselves (once a mom-to-be hits 35, she's more likely to have a multiple birth than a younger mother).

Expenses certainly jump when you have twins, or—*gasp*—triplets or more. You need twice (or thrice) the amount of diapers, formula, clothing, and gear. Plus, if you don't have family or friends nearby to help you—and you will need some help, especially during the first few months—you may have to hire a baby nurse, who'll charge you about 40% more than the going rate for a single baby.

Some financial help is available, though. If you're the parent of twins or more, you can take the initiative yourself by writing to companies that manufacture infant formula, bottles, and other baby products. Explain that you've just had a multiple birth. (Be sure to enclose copies of your babies' birth certificates.) At the very least, you'll get a free case of formula or a set of nipples and bottles. Other freebies that you might want to look for:

• Procter & Gamble offers coupons for a free package of diapers for each new baby when you deliver triplets or more. Call 800-285-6064.

- Many preschools and toddler play groups offer discounts when you enroll several children at the same time. Parochial schools often offer a declining fee structure, which means that you pay full price for the first one, and substantially less for each child enrolled thereafter.

- Public health service clinics often offer free immunizations for local residents. That could save you a bundle if you have to get shots for two or three kids.

- Mead Johnson, maker of Enfamil infant formulas, and Ross Laboratories, maker of rival Similac, give free formula to new parents of triplets or more through their local representatives. Ask your pediatrician about this offer.

For emotional support and more information about multiple births, contact the Triplet Connection, a nonprofit group that has the world's largest database on multiple births. Contact the group at: P.O. Box 99571, Stockton, CA 95209; 209-474-0885; www.inreach.com/triplets. To get in touch with a local support group in your area, contact Mothers of Supertwins, a national nonprofit group, at P.O. Box 951, Brentwood, NY 11717; 516-434-6678; www.mostonline.org. These support groups often hold sales at which families can buy and sell clothes and equipment from one another.

THE LESS GLAMOROUS GEAR

From the moment your child is born, he or she will be bombarded with hundreds of gizmos for being soothed to sleep, and thousands more to keep him or her stimulated (well, at least cooing and smiling) while awake. But a baby needs more. From birth, your daughter or son has a legal identity, which you, the parent, must tend to in the early years. For the most part, that means you have to provide a name and sign the birth certificate. But you also must get a Social Security number and make sure that your new dependent is covered under your medical insurance policy.

THE NAME GAME

You can call your child anything you like—even "Sue" if it's a boy—as long as it's a name and not a number (such as 99, for instance). Should you decide that the name doesn't fit, you can always change it. Generally, people don't change their names until they are adults, but sometimes parents do change their child's name, often after a divorce or remarriage. The laws vary by state. In some states, a simple affidavit signed by the parents is all that's needed. In other states, parents must show proof of an established new name, such as an insurance policy or marriage certificate.

Sometimes, a state will require a court order for a name change. You must petition the court first (depending on the state, that's the county probate court, superior court, or district court), and, in some cases, you must publish a notice of the name change in your local newspaper. Once the change is made officially, the court issues a "change of name order" or "decree." You'll then be handed either a brand-new birth certificate or a revised version of the original.

GETTING A BIRTH CERTIFICATE

This is a no-brainer for most parents. If the baby is born in a hospital or birthing center, a staff person will generally process the paperwork for you. All you have to do is provide the baby's name and some other pertinent information such as your name and your spouse's and your dates of birth. A preliminary form will be typed up, which you'll be asked to sign, and then it will be forwarded to your state's vital statistics division. (Check that form over carefully for typos or other errors before signing, however. It's easier to correct mistakes now than later on.) The real McCoy—complete with the baby's sex, weight, length, and exact time of arrival—will arrive at your home by mail in a few weeks. Store it in a safe spot like a safe-deposit box at the bank or a fireproof chest in the house. Obviously, you'll need this birth certificate to get Junior a passport, but you'll need it for more mundane matters, too, like registration for kindergarten or the local soccer team.

If you're planning a home birth, you'll probably have to fill these forms out on your own. Contact your state bureau of vital records for a birth certificate application. If you adopt a child, the child's name (that's the first and last name you've given him or her) is recorded in the adoption decree. A new birth certificate is then drawn up, in most states. This certificate replaces the original one, which is usually sealed with the adoption papers.

Applying for a Social Security Number

Whether your adorable six-month-old will be hitting the pavement as a baby model or opening up a savings account with funds from grandparents, he or she needs a Social Security number. In fact, even if the youngster does nothing more than eat, sleep, and go to school for the next 16 years, the child still needs a Social Security number. Why? The IRS now requires that each child whom you claim as a dependent on your income taxes must have his or her own number—or they will disallow the exemption. What if it's April 15th and you don't have a Social Security number yet for a child recently born into your family

whom you wish to claim as a dependent on your tax return? You must file for an extension. Once you receive the
child's Social Security number, you can then file your
taxes.

In most cases, it's easy to get a number. Many states now
let you apply for a Social Security card at the same time you
apply for a birth certificate. (That means the hospital will
process the paperwork for you.) If you don't apply for your
child's number at this time, however, you'll have to go to
your local Social Security office (look under the U.S. government listings in your phone book) or call the Social Security Administration's toll-free number: 800-772-1213. Ask
for form SS-5, the application for a Social Security number.
If you adopt an older child who already has a number, all
you have to do is register the name change with the Social
Security office. Again, either contact your local office or call
the 800 number.

UPDATING YOUR INSURANCE COMPANY'S FILES

Call your insurance company as soon as you can after your
baby is born. Each medical plan differs, but many insurers
nowadays insist that you notify them within 48 hours of the
birth or they won't provide any hospital coverage. (You
probably had to tell your insurer that you were pregnant
much earlier, too, so that your prenatal care was covered.
This postbirth call, however, should be made in addition to
any previous calls.) Generally, the insurer wants to know if
you delivered vaginally or by cesarean section and if the
baby suffered any complications. Was he born prematurely?
Does she have jaundice? When will you and the baby be re-
leased from the hospital?

Your baby should be covered automatically; there is no
waiting period. That isn't necessarily true if you adopt a

baby, however. Some insurers won't cover the child until the adoption has been finalized. That could be anywhere from a few months to a few years. Others offer coverage from the moment an adopted infant is placed with the family, but they exclude preexisting conditions. For more information, contact Adoptive Families of America, 3333 Highway 100-N, Minneapolis, MN 55422; 612-535-4829.

QUESTIONS AND ANSWERS

Q. What happens if there's a mistake on my baby's birth certificate?

A. You can't simply cross out the mistake and write in the correction. The procedure you must follow, however, depends on the state in which you live. In some states, additional forms must be filled out. Contact your state's department of vital records for more details. (See "For More Info.")

Q. My husband and I use different last names. Can we pick our baby's surname, or are their certain restrictions?

A. It depends on where you live. Babies used to be automatically given their father's last name whether the parents were married or not. Today, many women don't take their husband's name after marriage, so the issue is a bit more complex. Some states still insist that the father's surname be used if the parents are married. If the parents are not married, some states require that the mother's last name be used. Most states, however, do allow parents to use a hyphenated combination of their last names for their children. To make sure that your child's surname is legal in your state, contact your state's department of vital records. (See "For More Info.")

Q. A friend of mine insists that she picks up the best baby bargains at local garage sales. Is this a smart place to shop for baby stuff?

A. Occasionally. Clothes are often your best buys at garage, yard, or tag sales. Since most couples have just one or two children these days, the baby clothes don't wear out. Not only are these duds in good shape generally, but, like most yard sale items, they sell for 80% to 90% off their original cost. You'll find snowsuits priced at $3, overalls for a dollar. Big-ticket items are more difficult to assess. Carriages, cribs, and playpens abound at these sales, too, but they're often quite used. And you never know what you're getting from a safety standpoint. Might that sleigh-bed crib, for instance, be painted with leaded paint? Personally, I wouldn't buy a car seat at a yard sale, no matter how cheap it was. You can't really be sure that the seat is safe to use. And there's no way of testing it without putting your child at some risk.

Q. My grandmother says that she used to make infant formula from evaporated milk, which cost far less than store-bought formula. Is this a good idea?

A. Your grandmother may have fed her children homemade formula because it was as good as the best formula available at the time. But the new commercial formulas—which probably cost about three times the price of this homemade recipe—are so complete now that they closely resemble breast milk. No homemade formula can compare with that. At best, grandma's recipe ranks a distant third, nutritionally, behind breast-feeding and today's commercial formulas. If you're trying to cut costs, think seriously about nursing. It's the cheapest alternative. If you can't or don't want to breast-feed, use a commercial formula. Shortchanging your baby's health is not a good way to save money.

FOR MORE INFO

For questions concerning your child's legal name and/or birth certificate, contact your state's office of vital records:

Alabama
Vital Records
P.O. Box 5625
Montgomery, AL 36103-5625
334-613-5418

Alaska
Department of Health
   and Social Services
Bureau of Vital Statistics
P.O. Box 110675
Juneau, AK 99811-0675
907-465-3391

Arizona
Vital Records Office
P.O. Box 3887
Phoenix, AZ 85030
602-255-3260

Arkansas
Division of Vital Records
Arkansas Department
   of Health
4815 West Markham Street,
   Slot 44
Little Rock, AR 72205
501-661-2336

California
Department of Health
   Services
Vital Statistics Section
304 S Street
Sacramento, CA 95814
916-445-2684

Colorado
Vital Records
4300 Cherry Creek Drive
   South
Denver, CO 80246-1530
303-756-4464

Connecticut
Department of Public
   Health
Vital Records Section
410 Capitol Avenue,
   MF #11 VRS
P.O. Box 340308
Hartford, CT 06134

Delaware
Vital Statistics
P.O. Box 637
Dover, DE 19903
302-739-4721

District of Columbia
Vital Records Office
800 9th Street SW
Washington, DC 20024
202-645-5962

Florida
Vital Statistics
1217 Pearl Street
Jacksonville, FL 32202
904-359-6900

Georgia
Vital Records, Room 217-H
47 Trinity Avenue
Atlanta, GA 30334
404-656-4750

Hawaii
Vital Records Section
State Department of Health
P.O. Box 3378
Honolulu, HI 96801
808-586-4533

Idaho
Vital Statistics
P.O. Box 83720
Boise, ID 83720-0036
208-334-5988

Illinois
Division of Vital Records
State Department of Health
605 West Jefferson Street
Springfield, IL 62702-5097
217-782-6553

Indiana
State Department of Health
Section 3-D
Vital Statistics
2 North Meridean Street
Indianapolis, IN 46204
317-233-7030

Iowa
Iowa Department of Public
    Health
Vital Records
Lucas State Office Building
321 East 12th Street
Des Moines, IA 50319-0075
515-281-5871

Kansas
Vital Statistics
900 Southwest Jackson
    Street
Room 151
Topeka, KS 66612-2221
913-296-1400

Kentucky
Office of Vital Records
275 East Main Street
Frankfort, KY 40621
502-564-4212

Louisiana
Vital Records Registry
P.O. Box 60630
New Orleans, LA 70160
504-568-5152

Maine
Vital Records
Department of Human
    Services
221 State Street
Augusta, ME 04333-0011
207-287-3181

Maryland
Division of Vital Records
P.O. Box 68760
Baltimore, MD 21215
410-318-6119

Massachusetts
Registry of Vital Records
    and Statistics
470 Atlantic Avenue,
    2d Floor
Boston, MA 02210
617-753-8600

Michigan
Michigan Department of
  Community Health
Office of the State Registrar
  and Division of Health
  Statistics
P.O. Box 30195
Lansing, MI 48909
517-335-8656

Minnesota
Minnesota Department
  of Health
Vital Records
P.O. Box 9441
Minneapolis, MN 55440
612-623-5121

Mississippi
Vital Records
P.O. Box 1700
Jackson, MS 39215-1700
601-960-7981

Missouri
Department of Health
Vital Records
P.O. Box 570
Jefferson City, MO 65102
573-751-6387

Montana
Vital Records
P.O. Box 4210
Helena, MT 59604
406-444-4228

Nebraska
Vital Statistics
P.O. Box 95065
Lincoln, NE 68509-5065
402-471-2871

Nevada
Office of Vital Statistics
505 East King Street
Carson City, NV 89710
702-687-4480

New Hampshire
Vital Records
6 Hazen Drive
Concord, NH 03301
603-271-4654

New Jersey
Bureau of Vital Statistics
P.O. Box 370
Trenton, NJ 08625
609-292-4087

New Mexico
Vital Records
P.O. Box 26110
Santa Fe, NM 87502
505-827-2338

**New York (excluding
  New York City)**
State Department
  of Health
Vital Records Section
Empire State Plaza
Albany, NY 12237-0023
518-474-3075

New York City
New York City Department
  of Health
Vital Records
125 Worth Street
New York, NY 10013
212-788-4520

North Carolina
Vital Records
P.O. Box 29537
Raleigh, NC 27626
919-733-3526

North Dakota
Vital Records
State Capitol
600 East Boulevard
Bismarck, ND 58505-0200
701-328-2360

Ohio
Vital Statistics
Ohio Department of Health
P.O. Box 15098
Columbus, OH 43215-0098
614-466-2531

Oklahoma
Vital Records
State Department of Health
P.O. Box 53551
Oklahoma City, OK 73152
405-271-4040

Oregon
Vital Records
P.O. Box 14050
Portland, OR 97293
503-731-4095

Pennsylvania
Division of Vital Records
P.O. Box 1528
Room 401
Central Building
101 South Mercer Street
New Castle, PA 16101
412-656-3100

Rhode Island
Division of Vital Records
Health Department
3 Capitol Hill,
    Room 101
Providence, RI 02908-5097
401-222-2811

South Carolina
Department of Health
    and Environmental
    Control
Office of Vital Records
2600 Bull Street
Columbia, SC 29201
803-734-4810

South Dakota
Department of Health
Vital Records
445 East Capitol Avenue
Pierre, SD 57501
605-773-3355

Tennessee
Vital Records
421 Fifth Avenue North
Nashville, TN 37247-0350
615-741-1763

Texas
Bureau of Vital Statistics
P.O. Box 12040
Austin, TX 78711-2040
512-458-7111

Utah
Vital Records
P.O. Box 141012
Salt Lake City, UT 84114-
    1012
801-538-6105

Vermont
Vital Records
108 Cherry Street
P.O. Box 70
Burlington, VT 05402
802-863-7275

Virginia
Division of Vital Records
P.O. Box 1000
Richmond, VA 23208-1000
804-225-5000

Washington
Department of Health
Center for Health Statistics
P.O. Box 9709
Olympia, WA 98507-9709
360-753-5936

West Virginia
Vital Registration Office
Capitol Complex
Building 3, Room 516
Charleston, WV 25305
304-558-2931

Wisconsin
Vital Records
P.O. Box 309
Madison, WI 53701
608-266-1371

Wyoming
Vital Records
Hathaway Building
Cheyenne, WY 82002
307-777-7591

CHAPTER FOUR

The Juggling Act

Can you do it all? Do you want to?

Over the past decade, American parents have learned that "having it all"—the high-powered executive job, the perfect 2.5 children, the sprawling house in the suburbs—really means *doing* it all.

Have *you* thought yet how you're going to balance the demands of your job with those of your newly expanded family?

Some new parents assume that things will just fall into place after the baby is born. This rarely happens. Perhaps you expect to return to work full-time, for instance, six weeks after your daughter is born. But, when the time comes to return to work, you may not want to leave the baby so soon, and for so many hours. Or, perhaps the idea of dropping the baby off at a day care center across town every morning before you catch your commuter train sounded easier in theory. By week's end, you're exhausted.

You won't know how it feels to be a working parent until you *are* a working parent—and then it's often too late to set a plan in motion. (You'll probably be too tired at that point from juggling work and the baby to really investigate other options.) The key to happiness, if you will, is to plan ahead as much as possible. Think about what you want, and how much you're capable of doing. Can you take a six-month leave? How much of it will be a paid leave, if any? Can you reasonably just slide back into your old work routine? Do you work a lot of overtime? If you'd like to cut back on your hours—at least for the first year—could you? Does your firm allow flextime or job sharing? Can you afford to work less than full-time? Can you afford to stay at home? All of these questions must be answered to the best of your ability before you have the baby.

That's not to say, of course, that the decisions you make today can't be altered after that little bundle of joy arrives. It's just easier to do the legwork now. You'll have enough to do later on.

This chapter outlines the most popular flexible work arrangements along with the most common maternity/paternity leaves. You must find out if your employer offers any of these options. If not, don't be discouraged. Occasionally, somebody has to rock the boat. Why shouldn't it be you?

FLEXTIME

The traditional nine-to-five work schedule doesn't exactly jive with most children's routines. Most of their plays, soccer practices, and class visitations occur during the day when you're at work. Obviously, you can't be in two places at once, but you may be able to better juggle the demands of both if you can take advantage of *flextime*.

One of the most popular alternative work arrangements, flextime lets you vary your starting and quitting times as long as you work the required number of hours within a given time period. Some companies simply let you shift the standard workday forward or backward by one hour. Instead of working 9:00 A.M. to 5:00 P.M., you might work 8:00 to 4:00 or 10:00 to 6:00. Other employers, however, are more liberal. You must work during specific core hours—generally 10:00 A.M. to 2:00 P.M.—but you can start anytime after 7:00 A.M. and work up until 6:00 P.M.

Currently offered at thousands of government and private-sector jobs, flextime doesn't reduce your workload. It just gives you some leeway in either the morning or the late afternoon, so you can take a sick child to the doctor or applaud your student's efforts at the school science fair without taking time off from work.

Flextime works especially well when both spouses can take advantage of it. Let's assume that you both work from 9:00 A.M. until 5:00 P.M., for instance. You'll need child care for those eight hours (plus your commute time). However, if you both opt for flextime—one spouse works from 7:00 to 3:00; the other works from 10:00 to 6:00—your child could spend about three hours less each day with the babysitter.

A variation of flextime is the *compressed workweek*. Like flextime, this schedule doesn't cut your hours any. It simply rearranges them so that you can work a full-time routine in less than the typical five business days. Generally, you'll work four 10-hour days per week, but some professions, like nursing, let you work three 12-hour shifts per week.

With both flextime and a compressed workweek, you're not reducing your hours so you shouldn't be asked to take a cut in salary or benefits.

PART-TIME WORK

Feeling frazzled just *thinking* about managing a baby and working full-time? Perhaps you should consider working part-time. You'll cut back your hours on the job, and gain more time with the little one.

Ah, if only it were so simple. Many working parents (and child care experts) insist that part-time work gives mothers and fathers the best of both worlds. Trouble is, good-paying and career-advancing part-time slots are often tough to land.

Thumb through the want ads in this Sunday's paper, for instance, and you'll find a slew of part-time jobs available in the general labor market. But most of them—file clerk, receptionist, telemarketer—are low-paying, low-status jobs that don't offer medical insurance, pension plans, or other benefits. If your goal is just to make a few bucks while the kids are in school or if you're working more for the social contact than the money, these kinds of part-time jobs may be suitable for you.

If not, consider a second, and far more lucrative, alternative: Condense your current full-time job into a part-time position. Let's assume that you're an account executive at an advertising agency. If you were to handle just two clients (instead of the usual four), couldn't you get that job done in less time? In two and a half or three days? Since you'd be doing less work, you obviously wouldn't get paid your full salary anymore. Ideally, though, you'd still get paid *at the same rate*. If you work two-thirds of your old schedule, for instance, you'd get paid two-thirds of your former salary.

That's still less money than you were formerly earning, of course. But the difference may not be as great as you might think. Cut your work hours, and you cut your work-related expenses, too. If you work just three days per week, for example, you won't be spending as much on child care, lunches, clothing, dry cleaning, gasoline, parking, and/or other commuting costs as you did when you worked five days.

Your medical benefits, unfortunately, will generally be prorated along with your salary. If you're working two-thirds of your former schedule, you would receive two-thirds of the employer contribution toward your medical insurance premiums you received previously. The remainder would have to be purchased by you, unless you're covered by your spouse's policy and don't need it. Some employers may cut other benefits, such as life insurance, pension plan, or paid maternity leave, when you move to a part-time status.

Naturally you've got to get your boss (and probably the company) to agree to this arrangement. No small feat, unless you work for a company that already permits part-time work or at least other family-friendly alternatives. You have a better chance of succeeding if you have a job that can be broken into smaller pieces. Many of the creative professions (e.g., writing, photography, and graphic arts) let you pick your own assignments, for example, so that you can control your workload somewhat. Other vocations that are project-oriented, such as accounting and advertising, may allow this, too.

How many hours constitute part-time work? It depends. Generally, it's less than 35 hours but more than 10. If you're in a profession like law or medicine that routinely demands long hours—50, 60, even 70 hours per week—a 40-hour week may seem like part-time to you. Part-timers often work a full day, but fewer than five days per week. Or, they may still work five days per week, but fewer hours each day. It depends on what works for you and your employer.

One part-time option that's growing in popularity is *job sharing.* Under this arrangement, two employees "share" one full-time job. Each works part-time; they split the workload, salary, health benefits, and vacation. (Some companies, however, do offer full medical benefits to both workers.) Most job sharers work two and a half days per week, but some work five half-days per week or a full-time schedule every other week. Employers often prefer the job sharing option where somebody is always on the job to a straight part-time arrangement. Client calls don't go unanswered on Wednesday, for instance, because it's not your day to work. The trickiest part, often, is finding a partner with whom you can work easily.

CHECKLIST: VACATION DAYS, DISABILITY INSURANCE, AND OTHER DETAILS

Part-time work is perfect for some people. But, unless you iron out the details beforehand, you could be losing more than you realize. Find out the following facts first:

✔ *How will my base compensation be determined?* Your salary will probably be prorated according to the number of hours you work. But you might get paid by the hour. If it's the latter, find out if you get "overtime"—a higher rate for any hours you work beyond your scheduled part-time hours.

✔ *Will I still get periodic raises?* You should get regular salary increases, just as you would if you were working full-time. Don't fall for the argument that because you're working less than full-time your raise should be cut proportionately. If everyone else gets a 4% raise, you should, too.

✔ *Will I still get my year-end bonus?* If you got a bonus when you worked full-time, you should still get a bonus when you work part-time. (That's assuming, of course, that you have similar responsibilities.)

✔ *What benefits will I retain?* Generally, companies won't let you keep full-time benefits if you work part-time. Life insurance probably won't be provided, and your disability insurance may be cut back, too. If you need full medical coverage, try to negotiate that up front.

✔ *Do I get paid for Christmas?* Vacation days are usually tied to the amount of time you put in. If you work half of a full-time routine, you'll probably get half of the vacation days.

✔ *Can I work part-time permanently?* Some companies let you work part-time indefinitely. Others let you work a short-ened week for just a few months following your maternity leave.

TELECOMMUTING

Does working from home a day or two each week sound like a dream come true? Currently 8.4 million Americans do so, according to Link Resources, a market research firm in New York City. Of course, employees have always brought work home. But this is a more formal arrangement which allows you to work at home, or to *telecommute* by the use of an electronic linkup, *instead* of working at the office.

In recent years, more and more companies, such as Travelers-Aetna, Pacific Bell, U.S. West, and AT&T, have let employees set up shop at home. Naturally, technology has helped pave the way. Personal computers, software, modems, e-mail, even a video hookup that lets you hold teleconferences allow workers to handle increasingly complex tasks at home.

Jobs that involve research, writing, heavy telephone use, and little face-to-face interaction with clients or customers obviously lend themselves to a work-at-home arrangement. You can't put a fender on a car at home, for instance, or take a patient's blood pressure. But most traditional office or professional jobs entail some autonomous work that can be done at home one or two days per week, which is about how much time you can expect to telecommute. Few people who hold corporate jobs work from home full-time.

Parents often love this setup because it gives them more time with the kids. While working at home is no substitute for paid child care (you simply wouldn't believe how many people assume I write with one hand and hold the baby with the other) you'll save the time you'd normally spend commuting. What's more, since most at-home workers claim they're more productive because they waste less time in meetings and idle chatter around the watercooler, you probably could work an abbreviated schedule and still get the same amount of work done.

Mostly, being at home makes you more accessible. You can take your child to the doctor without taking half a day off to do it, or work through your lunch hour and go to your youngster's soccer practice at 4:00 in the afternoon. Depending on the arrangement you've struck with your boss, you could even quit work two or three hours early during the day, as long as you put in those hours later once the kids are tucked in for the night.

HOW TO NEGOTIATE A WORK-AT-HOME ARRANGEMENT

"How will I know you're not doing the laundry?" Don't be surprised if that's how your boss responds when you ask to work at home every Monday. Unfortunately, managers are still wary of this work-at-home concept because it means they have less control over you. They also fear it may mean more work for them. To quell your boss's anxieties, clearly spell out what you want and how you plan to do it—in writing, since it's harder to convince people unless they can see it on paper. Plus, having it in black and white circumvents the classic "I thought" syndrome, as in "I thought it was understood that I would no longer be responsible for that client" or "I thought I didn't have to attend the Monday morning staff meeting anymore."

Some points to include in your proposal:

- Pitch your request in terms of how the company—and not just you—will benefit. Point out, for instance, that you'll be able to provide extended hours of telephone coverage by working earlier or later hours at home. Note that many companies cut their overhead expenses when employees work at home.

- Cite examples of similar arrangements either in your department or within the organization itself. If you're truly breaking new ground, point to examples at other companies.

- Decide what work will be done at home. And figure out how that work will be evaluated. Will you have a monthly progress report, for instance?

- Set up a schedule. Can you set up your own hours, as long as the work gets done? Or, must you be reachable during core hours, say 10:00 A.M. to 3:00 P.M.? Iron out which meetings you'll attend, and how accessible you must be for emergencies.

- Figure out what equipment you'll need. At the very least, you'll need a separate phone line and a computer with a modem. Will the company pick up the tab?

- Make sure your salary and benefits remain intact. Since you're still a full-time employee, you shouldn't be asked to forfeit any benefits; that includes your health insurance, pension plan, sick days, vacation days, and company holidays.

- Determine the duration of the arrangement. Is it going to be temporary, or longer-term? Your best bet: Offer to work at home on a pilot basis for, say, three months. That way, you and your boss can get out of the deal gracefully, if it's not working.

MATERNITY AND PATERNITY LEAVES

Kathryn Mulvihill took six months off with pay after her son Timothy was born. Fortunately, her employer, a German-based reinsurance firm, cut her a generous deal: 15 paid weeks of maternity leave, plus 2 weeks of vacation and 30 unused sick days that had accrued since she'd joined the firm 13 years earlier. Jackie Epstein wasn't so lucky. A cable television producer, she received six weeks of disability pay—equal to a fraction of her normal salary—after she gave birth to her third child, Andrew. For the remaining six weeks she took off, Epstein had to use up her vacation time, and, for two weeks, go unpaid entirely.

Why the disparity? Maternity/paternity leaves vary widely from one employer to another. While recent legislation such as the Family and Medical Leave Act of 1993 has en-abled more parents to take time off to tend their newborns, how much you get—and for how long—still depends largely on the policies your employer has in place. Some compa-nies, like Mulvihill's, offer generous, enlightened packages; others, like Epstein's, have so-so deals.

Various types of leaves—both paid and unpaid—are of-fered by employers across the country. Obviously, the best time to ask questions about how much you're entitled to and what types of benefits you can expect is before your child arrives on the scene.

DISABILITY LEAVE

You may hear some new mothers say that they're out on *dis-ability* from their job. That's simply the way that many em-

ployers offer maternity leave. Under the Pregnancy Discrimination Act of 1978, employers (of 15 employees or more)
who have short-term disability policies must treat pregnancy
like any other disability. (Employers don't have to offer disability leaves at all, but most do.) A company that allows a
six-week leave for a worker with an injured back or a broken
leg, for instance, must grant the same time off to a woman
who has just given birth. In effect, this law simply extends to
pregnant women the same benefits already in place for
other workers.

Disability leaves are generally paid. How much one gets
usually depends on length of service with the company and,
often, job rank. Some disability leaves, however, are unpaid,
or only partially paid. Part-timers, for instance, frequently
aren't eligible for disability leave.

Depending on an employer's policy, medical benefits may
be continued, reduced, or stopped altogether during a disability leave. Job reinstatement or job protection (the
promise of a comparable job rather than the same job held
previously) may or may not be guaranteed. However, if
other employees who take disability leaves are guaranteed
to get their jobs back on returning to work, so should a
pregnant woman.

Some companies offer very generous disability leaves.
They hold your job, pay your benefits in full, and let you
take off up to 26 weeks at 60% pay. However, you may not
medically need such an extended leave; if your doctor says
you're physically capable of returning to work at eight weeks
postpartum, you won't qualify for any disability benefits beyond that point. Should you decide to stay out on leave a bit
longer anyway (without pay), the law no longer protects
your job or salary.

How much time off is generally taken? For a normal pregnancy, doctors usually recommend a six- to eight-week leave;

for a cesarean section, an additional two weeks. Since a disability leave is granted because of a medical condition (i.e., pregnancy and delivery), most new fathers and adoptive parents don't qualify.

PARENTAL LEAVE

Some companies offer *parental* leave instead of disability leave. Such policies generally apply to fathers and adoptive parents as well as to mothers. Parental leaves usually have the same maximum duration as disability leaves (six to eight weeks) and may be a combination of paid and unpaid time.

Parental leave for new dads has been hotly debated in this era of equal-opportunity parenthood. But, unfortunately, it has failed to really take hold. Certainly more men than in the past now use the growing number of leave programs that employers offer, but far fewer men use them than women. At AT&T, for instance, one man for every 20 women took family leave in 1997, up from 1 in every 400 in 1982.

It seems that men still fear taking a paternity leave will make them appear soft in their commitment to work and prevent advancement. And at a time of continued downsizing, global competition, and demands from investors, most corporate dads face growing pressures at the office. (Of course, working moms face similar pressures, and it hasn't stopped them from taking maternity leaves.)

Proponents of extended leave for men say research shows that babies benefit greatly from time spent with fathers, and that the experience helps strengthen families. But the realities of corporate and family life can't always take those ideals into consideration.

UNPAID LEAVE

If you want to spend the first few months with your newborn but your job offers just a six-week maternity leave, you may still be able to wangle some extra time off. These days, more and more companies are offering *unpaid* leaves that guarantee the same or a comparable job on returning to work, in addition to paid leaves. Frequently, such companies will offer a standard, paid maternity leave of six to eight weeks; after that, the new mother can take an unpaid leave of three, six, or 12 months.

In many cases, federal law now dictates that employees be allowed to take some unpaid leave after the birth or adoption of a child. Under the Family and Medical Leave Act of 1993, for instance, employers of 50 employees or more must grant female and male workers up to 12 weeks of unpaid leave, per year, for the birth or adoption of a child. (You can also take a leave to care for a sick child or an elderly dependent.)

CHECKLIST: NEGOTIATING YOUR MATERNITY LEAVE

Before breaking the good news to your boss, find out about maternity leave options. That way, should you be asked about your postbaby work plans, you can discuss them intelligently. Most of this information can be gleaned from your employee handbook (if your company has one) or from conversations with your labor representative or human resources or personnel director. Colleagues who are young fathers or mothers may also be helpful.

Whether you plan on taking a paid or an unpaid leave, or both, find out:

✔ Am I eligible for disability or maternity leave? (Some companies grant leaves only after you've been employed with the firm for a certain amount of time.)

✔ How long will my paid leave be?

✔ Will I receive full pay, or partial payment?

✔ When will I begin receiving the checks?

✔ Can I extend my leave by using vacation time or unused sick time?

✔ How do I submit a leave request?

✔ Will my current job, or a comparable one, be held for me?

✔ Does that job guarantee change depending on the length of my leave?

✔ Will my benefits continue during a paid leave? An unpaid leave? If not, will the company let me pay for them?

✔ Will I lose seniority? Upon my return, will I still be eligible for my annual raise and/or bonus?

✔ Who will do my work while I'm gone?

✔ Can I return to work at a less than full-time schedule, at least initially?

✔ Can I take advantage of flextime, job sharing, or telecommuting options?

✔ If I take an unpaid leave, can I afford to live on no salary? (Obviously, you'll have to answer this last question yourself.)

QUESTIONS AND ANSWERS

Q. My wife and I are expecting our first child next month. My employer does offer parental leave, and I'd really like to take some time off. But I'm afraid it will hurt my chances of getting promoted. How can I tell if this will be held against me, careerwise?

A. If you're asking for a guarantee, there isn't one. You could just take the leave that you're allotted—provided you can afford to take that much time off without pay—and let the chips fall where they may. You could talk to your boss, who may, in confidence, admit that it would be a bad sign for you take off for three months. Or, you can do what a lot of other working dads do. They arrange a short, unofficial leave, which they're careful not to label as time off with a child. Generally, it's only about six days, a combination of vacation days and sick time.

Q. I've heard many people say that you can't have it all—at least not all at one time. What do they mean by that?

A. Some experts argue that you can't tend to young children properly and work full throttle at your career simultaneously. After all, no matter how hard you work or how organized you are, there are still only 24 hours in a day. These experts believe that you need to "sequence" your family and work commitments throughout your life. In other words, downshift your career involvement when your children are young (and they need you the most) and then gradually accelerate your career commitments as your children mature and leave the nest. It's a nice theory, but it's not always easy to put into practice.

FOR MORE INFO

Contact the *Equal Employment Opportunity Commission* if you want to know more about the Pregnancy Discrimination Act of 1978: 800-669-3362.

The *Women's Bureau of the U.S. Department of Labor* offers a booklet called "State Maternity and Family Leave Laws," which explains the leave laws in each state. The Bureau also can provide information on the various flexible work options available. Contact the Bureau at: 200 Constitution

Avenue NW, Room South 3305, Washington, DC 20210; 202-219-6606; 800-347-3741.

Catalyst, a national research and advisory organization, works with corporations to promote the career and leadership development of women. Many of Catalyst's publications are aimed at helping women balance work and family. Contact Catalyst at: 120 Wall Street, 5th Floor, New York, NY 10005; 212-514-7600.

CHAPTER FIVE

$

Who's Minding the Children?

My oldest son practically leapt through the door of his nursery school this morning. My youngest barely said good-bye; he was too busy playing "this little piggy" with the baby-sitter. Yet, no matter how happy they seem, I never feel exactly right about leaving my kids in someone else's care. It's my job to take care of them, after all. Unfortunately, it's also my job to earn a living.

Whether you and your spouse are both going back to work, or you're just catching a film and a quick bite on Saturday night, you'll need someone to watch the children. For the latter, you can probably enlist Grandma's help (for nothing), or a teenager down the street who'll charge you from $3 to $10 per hour. If you both must—or want to—return to work, you'll need to find a more permanent child care arrangement.

The options available for either part-time or full-time child care vary widely, as do quality and price. In years past, of course, most of us would have looked to our mothers or aunts or sisters to help us out. (I'm not being sexist here; most of the child rearing in this country has been and is still done predominantly by women.) Securing a friend or relative's help is, for some people, still a viable (and, often, the cheapest) option. But in many cases, our relatives live too far away nowadays, or they hold down jobs outside the home, too. As a result, you must pay a stranger to tend to your little ones while you're at the office.

How much will that cost you, and what kind of service can you expect? The answers depend largely on the type of care you choose and where you live. (Child care, like almost everything else, just costs more in a big city than in a small town.) In general, you have three choices: *in-home care* provided by a nanny, au pair, or baby-sitter; *family day care,* in which your child (and several others) are cared for in someone else's home; and *group day care* offered to a group of children by a church, community center, or business.

None of these options are perfect, nor are they all available in every neighborhood across the country. And, what works now for your three-month-old daughter may not be appropriate when she's two years old. Normally, one fact you can be assured of, however: Unless Grandma is watching the little one gratis, child care is by far the biggest expense you'll incur during your child's early years.

CHILD CARE OPTIONS

IN-HOME CARE

When both parents work, they often hire a "parent substitute"—either nanny, au pair, baby-sitter, or housekeeper—to mind the kids while they're away. Some experts feel this is the best type of care for a very young child because the tot gets individual attention in the familiar comfort of his or her own home. Unfortunately, it's the most expensive care, too. Many parents prefer this arrangement because they get to call the shots. The in-home caregiver works for you. That means you set the hours, the pay, and the job's duties. In return, you must pay taxes and file the necessary paperwork on your employee. (See "Taxes, Insurance, and Other Complicated Stuff" section later in the chapter for more details.)

Parents frequently assume that all in-home caregivers are "nannies"—especially those who live with the family. But that isn't necessarily so. Generally, a nanny is a child care specialist. While she may not arrive on your doorstep via a flying umbrella, a good nanny is schooled in early childhood education, nutrition, and cardiopulmonary resuscitation (CPR). Professionally trained nannies cost $300 to $400 per week ($600 in Manhattan and Los Angeles) plus room and board.

An au pair, meanwhile, is generally a European girl aged 18 to 25 who wants to visit the United States. In exchange for her room and board and a small weekly salary, an au pair will take care of your kids for up to 45 hours per week. In 1997, the minimum salary set up by the government was $139.05 per week, but this arrangement isn't as cheap as it appears. Most of the au pair programs charge you a one-time program fee of about $4,500, which covers the au pair's round-trip airfare, her medical insurance for a year, and training. What's more, an au pair's visa—by law—is valid for only one year, so this is not a long-term setup. At year's end, you'll have to find another au pair (and pay another program fee) or find some other child care arrangements. In general, an au pair does cost less than a nanny, but she may or may not have prior experience caring for children.

A baby-sitter isn't a professional caregiver. (Typically, it's just a way to earn money while finishing school.) A sitter often has little or no formal training for the job, but may have lots of hands-on experience. You can pay by the hour. A housekeeper, on the other hand, cleans your home, does the marketing, and cooks the meals, and will provide some child care: get the kids on and off the school bus, for instance, or shuttle them back and forth to baseball practice and violin lessons. But that's not the main responsibility. A housekeeper, à la Alice of "The Brady Bunch" or Mr. Belvedere, is best suited for school-age children.

The cost of in-home care varies widely across the country. As a general rule, however, expect it to cost about three times as much as a child care center in your area. The gap between in-home care and out-of-home care narrows, however, if you have two or more kids. Most centers charge per child. They may cut you a better deal if you enroll your twins. But, unless your youngsters are close in age, it's unlikely they'd all go to the same day care program. Nannies generally don't charge much more for three children than for two (unless two of those children are infant twins; nannies *do* charge more for that).

The type of care your child receives will depend on the individual caregiver and how you manage that person as an employee. Why does the caregiver work as a nanny, for instance? Does she truly love children, or are her career options somewhat limited? Are the hours too long? Is the caregiver expected to cook and clean and take care of two very young children?

ADVANTAGES:

- Your child gets lots of individual attention.

- Your child is in familiar surroundings—own bed, high chair, and toys.

- The child follows his or her own schedule for meals and naps.

QUESTIONS TO ASK A PROSPECTIVE NANNY OR OTHER IN-HOME CAREGIVER

- What experience have you had taking care of children?
- What was your last job, and why did you leave it?
- Why are you interested in this job?
- How long do you envision staying with this job?
- Do you have children of your own? If so, who takes care of them while you work?
- Do you have any special training in CPR or first aid?
- How do you plan on spending your day with my child?
- What types of activities would you do? What rainy-day activities?
- Where and how often would you take my child outside to play?
- Can you swim, ride a bike, and take part in most physical activities?
- Would you welcome a play date with another child and caregiver if I arranged it?
- How do you generally discipline a child of this age?
- How will you travel to work each week? What happens if it rains or snows?
- What days or holidays would you expect to have off?
- What would you do if the baby cried for an hour?
- How would you handle an emergency?
- What would you do if the baby was sick? If you were sick?
- Can you read and write in English? Are you fluent in any other languages?
- Do you smoke, drink alcohol, or take a prescribed medication?
- Have you ever been arrested or convicted of any crime?
- Have you ever been institutionalized for a physical or psychological illness?
- Do you have an American driver's license? A valid passport and work visa?
- What is your Social Security number?

- There's no need to make special arrangements when your child is sick.

- You set the hours—especially important if you start work very early or work overtime.

- If you have older children, too, the caregiver can take care of them when they come home from school and when school is closed for vacations and holidays.

- Infants and toddlers benefit from less exposure to germs.

DISADVANTAGES:

- In-home care is the most expensive form of care.

- There's no backup if your caregiver is sick or quits.

- No licensing is required for in-home care, so it's hard to determine quality, especially if your child doesn't speak yet.

- You must arrange some peer group activities. Otherwise, your child could be isolated from other kids.

- Family loses some privacy if caregiver lives in.

- Parents must pay taxes and file paperwork for the caregiver.

FAMILY DAY CARE

Many parents like the homey feel of this extended-family arrangement. Your child, in most cases, is cared for by another mother in her home. Often, she'll be tending her own or another family's young children, too—up to a maximum of five or six kids. This type of caregiver may take babies as young as six weeks old, and may concentrate on a certain age group—perhaps three years old and under—while frequently also watching older children during after-school hours and school holidays and vacations. Generally flexible about hours, this caregiver may watch your kids for two or five days per week, for 10 hours per day or just until nap time. The fee, which can be as little as $75 per week, may include lunch and a snack.

You'll find all levels of expertise under this arrangement—and hardly any regulation. Typically, a mother may start a family day care in her home because it's a way to earn money while caring for her own brood. She may or may not be a licensed caregiver. Even in those states where a license or certificate is required to operate such a business, not every family day care complies with those rules. The fact that a day care is registered, certified, or licensed (the terms used vary from state to state and can mean different things) doesn't necessarily guarantee the quality will be higher. What it does mean, however, is that the day care meets certain health and safety guidelines, such as the number of children who can be cared for and the proper placement of fire extinguishers and smoke alarms. That's very reassuring to most parents, so expect to pay more for a licensed caregiver than an unlicensed one.

In this category, you might also find something called *group family day care*. It's the same kind of care basically, except on a larger scale. The caregiver, with an assistant or another full-fledged caregiver, may be tending up to 12 children.

One final consideration: Unlike an in-home child care arrangement, you're not the boss in this situation. The provider is an entrepreneur running a very small business. A service is offered; you buy it. If you don't like the methodology or you feel the kids watch too much television, you don't have much say in the matter. That's how the business is run. In most cases, you just have to accept it, or look elsewhere.

QUESTIONS TO ASK A PROSPECTIVE FAMILY DAY CARE PROVIDER

- How long have you been caring for children in your home?
- How many other children do you care for now? How old are they?
- Do you have your own children? How old are they? Are they at home, or in school?
- Who else is home in the house during the day?
- Are you licensed to run a family day care?
- Do you work alone, or with an assistant?
- Do you have any special training in child care, first aid, or CPR?
- Where do the children play, eat, and nap?
- Are meals and snacks provided?
- What items would I need to bring from home, such as bottles, formula, diapers, and toys?
- How frequently do the children go out, and where do they go?
- What happens if I get stuck working overtime and have to pick my child up an hour later?
- Do you have any backup plan if you're sick?
- Do you have any pets?
- What do you do if a child misbehaves?
- What kinds of activities are available for the children?
- How much TV are they allowed to watch?
- How often do you read to the children?
- What is a typical day like?

ADVANTAGES:

- The atmosphere is warm and homelike.

- Flexible hours may be offered.

- Usually it is less expensive than either in-home care or group day care.

- Your child will have ready playmates.

- Smaller group size often appeals to young children.

- Older siblings may be cared for during after-school hours.

- Provider may care for infants under three months old. (Many group centers don't.)

DISADVANTAGES:

- Family day care provider often has less training in child development (if any) than other child care providers.

- Many family day cares won't let you bring a sick child.

- There may be no backup if the provider gets sick.

- Not as well-regulated as group day care, many family day cares are unlicensed and therefore may not adhere to prescribed health and safety regulations.

GROUP DAY CARE

Under this arrangement, your child is cared for by a staff of trained, experienced teachers and aides in a "center" (that's anyplace outside the home setting), along with other similarly aged children. Typically operated by a church, synagogue, community center, government agency, or business, these centers handle large groups of children, ranging from at least 15 kids to 50 or more.

A more formal and elaborate setup than family day care, most group centers are fully stocked with arts and crafts supplies, blocks, dolls, and other toys, as well as out-

QUESTIONS TO ASK A PROSPECTIVE GROUP DAY CARE PROVIDER

- How long has the center been open?
- Are you licensed?
- What are the qualifications of the staff?
- What is the usual staff-to-child ratio?*
- What is the minimum number of adults who will be on hand on any given day?
- What's the turnover of the staff like? How many of the current staff have been working here for a year or more?
- What hours and days is the center open?
- How much extra do you charge for extended hours?
- For what holidays does the center close?
- How many children currently attend the center? What's the limit?
- Is anyone on staff trained in first aid?
- What kind of insurance do you have?
- How many meals and snacks are provided, and what do you typically provide?
- What hospital emergency room is used if my child needs immediate medical treatment?
- Do the children go outside every day? Where?
- Are there any field trips? Will I be notified in advance if my child is going on such a trip?
- Do I get a discount if I have more than one child enrolled in the center?
- How do you discipline children?
- What types of activities will my child be doing?
- Are the children separated by age group?
- Will you toilet train my child?
- Can children play by themselves at certain times during the day, or are they always expected to be part of the group?

- Is there a quiet area for naps, or a specific rest time during the day?
- Do you read to the children?
- Do you give written progress reports or have regular parent conferences?
- Can I visit the center without giving you prior notice?

If you have an infant, ask:

- How frequently are diapers changed?
- Will my baby be kept in a crib all day?
- Will you talk to my baby during diaper changing or feeding?
- How many people will be taking care of my child?
- How long will it be before someone picks up a baby who is crying?

*The American Academy of Pediatricians recommends one adult to three children under 24 months, four children 25 to 30 months, five children 31 to 35 months, or seven three-year-olds.

door slides, swings, and jungle gyms. Each day's planned social and educational activities are geared to your child's age and development. An occasional field trip to the local post office or firehouse is undertaken. Three-year-olds, for instance, may paint or work with clay, put on a puppet show, and run around in the playground—all before noon. After lunch, they may listen to stories and settle down for a nap.

A group center will mostly likely be properly licensed and insured and meet the minimum health and safety standards set by the state. Because it's monitored more closely than family day care, the cost is a bit steeper: $100 to $200 per week. Most centers offer full days only; they open at 6:00 or 7:00 A.M. and often close by 6:00 P.M. But some places do offer partial day or after-hours arrangements. A few companies now offer on-site group day care centers for their employees' children. Ideally, this means that you'd take your baby to work with you, drop the little one off at the center, have a visit at lunchtime, and take your baby home with you.

A group center can be a very reliable form of child care, because if a teacher or aide is sick, the center finds a replacement (it's not your headache). And, an increasing number of centers now care for babies as young as six weeks old.

ADVANTAGES:

- Care is always available—even if a teacher gets sick or quits.

- Staff is generally better trained in child development.

- Group centers have a greater variety of equipment, materials, and activities on hand.

- Usually some type of educational program is offered, too.

- Most such centers are regulated and must meet basic safety and health standards.

DISADVANTAGES:

- Group centers usually operate only during normal business hours and may be closed for certain holidays.

- Some children have problems interacting with such a large group.

- Group day care is usually more expensive than family day care.

- Children generally are cared for by more than one caregiver, so they have less chance to bond with one person in particular.

- High staff turnover is likely, due to long hours and low wages.

- Not all centers will care for infants under three months of age.

THE BOTTOM LINE

One type of child care isn't inherently better than another. What matters most, ultimately, is the *quality* of the care, not the type of care itself. And that quality will depend on what's available in your neck of the woods, what you and your child need specifically, and how much money you can spend. (See Figure 5.1.) In-home care, as you've seen, is probably the most expensive option. It isn't unreasonable to expect to pay a good nanny at least $300 per week, plus room and board and, in many cases, paid vacations and sick time. But it's often the next best thing to being there yourself.

Group day care, meanwhile, may run you far less, just $150 per week in some cases; family day care, as little as $75. Under these out-of-your-home arrangements, your

FIGURE 5.1 AT A GLANCE: THE COST OF CHILD CARE

TYPE OF CHILD CARE	AVERAGE COST	ESTIMATED COST FOR YOUR FAMILY
Nanny	$250–$600*	
Au pair	$139.05*	
Family day care	$75–$125	
Group day care	$100–$200	
Occasional babysitter	$3–$10/hr.	

*Doesn't include room and board.

child gets to play with other children, and generally will have a host of activities appropriate to his or her age and development to pick from. But there will be a group of children vying for the caregiver's attention. Some kids thrive in a large, busy environment; others need more personalized attention.

Most group day cares work standard business hours. They may provide after-hours service, even a bus that picks up and drops off your youngster every day, but you'll pay extra for that. Family day care and in-home care generally offer more flexible scheduling, especially if you set it up in advance that on Tuesdays and Thursdays you have to work late. If either of these providers becomes sick, however, you'll be stranded unless you have a backup arrangement. Group centers provide their own backup support, but due to low wages and long hours these places are frequently understaffed.

If you were expecting a neat answer, I'm afraid there isn't one. This is one time where you may have to rely on your gut instincts. Do you trust the caregiver? Does the place feel right to you? Could you easily picture your child thriving in such a situation?

FINDING THAT SPECIAL SOMEONE

Uncovering a quality child care arrangement takes time and energy. Some lucky parents find the perfect nanny or center the first time out, and that arrangement lasts until their child goes to grade school. Others, like me, use a handful of different sitters, centers, and programs until they hit upon the perfect (or as near-perfect as you're ever going to get) setup. Here's how to find a situation that will work for you:

1. *Ask around.* (And I mean *around.*) Ask your friends, neighbors, relatives, and coworkers for leads and/or recommendations. Ask your children's pediatrician and your obstetrician. Talk to parents of other kids wherever

you are: at the playground, school, the park, the Little League game on Saturday. Contact your church, synagogue, YMCA, or local recreation center. The more people you talk to, the greater your chances of finding a suitable child care situation.

2. *Advertise.* Run a classified ad in your local newspaper or advertiser. (Be sure to search the ads yourself: Sometimes caregivers in need of work run ads.) Post a help wanted notice on the bulletin board at your grocery store or the employment office of the local college. In your ad, include the hours needed, the number of children to be cared for and their ages, and a phone number to call. Be explicit about the qualifications needed: If you want someone with five years' experience, say so.

3. *Get professional help.* There are employment agencies that specialize in placing housekeepers or nannies. Most often they place full-time help, but it could be a live-in or live-out arrangement. Expect to pay a fee for this service: typically, two to four weeks of the caregiver's salary. The American Council of Nanny Schools offers a list of schools that have met the Council's training criteria. Some of the schools offer placement services. Au pairs can be found through government-authorized programs. (See "For More Info" section.)

4. *Size 'em up, face-to-face.* When hiring in-home help, you must ask a prospective candidate to visit you and the kids in your home. (If you're running an ad, do some preliminary screening over the phone. Obviously, you can't see in person everyone who calls.) The purpose of the meeting is to find out more about the applicant's background and experience. (See questions on page 91.) But you also want to look for subtle clues about the kind of person the candidate is. Did she genuinely seem to like children,

smile a lot, ask your preschooler about Big Bird, shake a rattle or make a goofy face for your six-month-old?

If you're choosing a center—either a family variety or the group type—visit the site. Observe what's going on between the kids and the caregiver(s). Look for cleanliness, an assortment of toys and activities, and a kid-friendly environment with enough space for young arms and legs to move about. Are the children at the center happily occupied, or squabbling in the block pile? Does the outdoor equipment look sturdy?

5. *Check out references—thoroughly.* Even if your best friend recommended a family day care mom, or the woman at the agency swears she's checked and double-checked your prospective nanny, you must verify a caregiver's background yourself. Other people's standards may not be up to yours. And other people often just don't ask the right questions. To find out if a reference is valid (some caregivers do give bogus references to make it look like they have experience), ask questions that require more than a yes or no answer, such as, "When did she work for you? What were her duties? Why was her service no longer needed? Would you hire her back?"

6. *Build a relationship slowly.* It's best to let child and caregiver get acquainted over a series of shorter meetings. If possible, have your child be at a new day care center for only a few hours each day for the first week or so, until comfortable with the new surroundings. Have a new nanny spend at least one full day with you and your baby to learn how you do things and get a feel for your child's routine. Again, if possible, ease this transition by leaving the two alone for short periods of time, gradually lengthening your time away as their relationship develops.

TAXES, INSURANCE, AND OTHER COMPLICATED STUFF

When you hire an in-home caregiver, you're supposed to pay taxes on those wages and file certain forms with the government. This is such an expensive, time-consuming process, though, that an estimated three-quarters of these payments aren't reported. Parents simply pay their in-home caregivers in cash, or "off the books." That saves them money—probably 10% to 20% of the nanny's salary—and time in preparing all those documents. But it's against the law. If detected (the Internal Revenue Service does seem to be cracking down on more of these cases), you would generally be hit with a severe fine. And you can just kiss your plan of running for attorney general good-bye.

To keep it legal, here's what you have to do:

PAY SOCIAL SECURITY AND MEDICARE TAXES

If you pay your in-home caregiver $50 or more within three months' time, you must pay Social Security and Medicare taxes on those wages. Both you and the nanny pay a portion. In 1996, for example, you each were asked to pay 6.2% for Social Security and 1.45% for Medicare. These tax payments must be made every quarter. You can ask your baby-sitter to send her own contribution in, but if he or she forgets to do so (or just chooses not to), the government will hold you responsible later on for payment of those back taxes—and charge you a penalty as well. Many employers, therefore, either foot the entire tax bill themselves or deduct the employees' shares from their pay and send the employees' contributions in with their own. If you do pay both parts, you must list the employee share as additional taxable income on your employee's W-2 form at the end of the year.

WITHHOLD FEDERAL INCOME TAX

You don't have to withhold federal income taxes from wages paid to a nanny. But you can, if the nanny wants you to and you agree. (The nanny must then sign Form W-4, Employee's Withholding Allowance Certificate.) To find out how much to withhold, use the income tax tables provided by the IRS in Publication 15, "Circular E, Employer's Tax Guide."

PAY UNEMPLOYMENT AND WORKERS' COMPENSATION

If you pay your in-home caregiver $1,000 or more within three months' time, you must pay Federal Unemployment Tax Act (FUTA) tax on those wages. You—not your nanny—must pay this tax. The current rate (1997) is 6.2%. You report payments to the IRS using Form 940 (or 940-EZ). Some states require you to pay a state unemployment tax, too. Often, if you must pay the state, you'll get a lower federal tax rate. Contact your state's unemployment tax agency for more information.

The laws governing workers' compensation vary from state to state. This insurance, which covers you should your caregiver get hurt while working in your home, may be required even if your nanny doesn't live in your home. In some cases, you may be covered for workers' compensation under your homeowner's insurance policy. In some states, though, you must have a separate workers' compensation policy. (Your insurance agent should be able to give you more information about this.)

FILE THESE DOCUMENTS

You'll need an employer identification number (not the same as your Social Security number) to report the taxes paid for employees. You use Form SS-4 to obtain the number. (Obviously, you only have to fill out this form once.) Every quarter, you'll have to fill out Form 942 for Social Security and Medicare. Once per year, you'll have to fill out Form 940 (or 940-EZ) for unemployment tax, and Form W-2, which reports your employee's yearly earnings. You give a copy of the W-2 to your employee and another to the Social Security Administration. (If you have more than one employee, you must use Form W-3, Transmittal of Wage and Tax Statements, to send the Forms W-2 to the Social Security Administration.) When you file your own income tax return, you'll need to attach Schedule H to your regular Form 1040 (or 1040A).

For the most up-to-date information on all reporting requirements, call the IRS (800-829-3676/800-TAX-FORM) for two booklets: "Child and Dependent Care Expenses" (Publication 503) and "Household Employer's Tax Guide" (Publication 926). The IRS will answer specific questions on the tax hot line (800-829-1040/800-TAX-1040).

MAKE SURE YOUR NANNY HAS A GREEN CARD

Legally, you can hire only American citizens or foreigners who are authorized to work in the United States. And you can't just take a nanny's word for it. As an employer, you must verify the nanny's eligibility by completing the Immigration and Naturalization Service Form I-9, Employment Eligibility Verification. Both you and the nanny must sign the form. You must also see proof of eligibility of employment: That could be a Social Security card, a U.S. passport, or an alien registration card. For copies of the form and more information, contact the U.S. Department of Justice, Immigration and Naturalization Service, at 800-755-0777.

CHECK OUT YOUR CAR INSURANCE

Your caregiver who will be driving the kids in your car may have to be added to your auto insurance policy. Ask your insurance agent about your state's requirements.

QUESTIONS AND ANSWERS

Q. I'd like to hire a nanny. Do I have to pay for holidays and vacation time?

A. No, but you should. A nanny is your full-time employee and, like you, needs a vacation every year. For the first year, I'd offer one or two weeks paid. Many families ask that the nanny take vacation when they take their vacation. (You don't have to worry about finding substitute care that way.) But if you want the nanny to accompany you on your vacation to take care of the children, you'll have to let the nanny take a vacation at another time. Even though your family is vacationing, your nanny is still working! Holidays are another matter. Unless there's some conflict of interest (you take off for Passover; the nanny wants Good Friday off) I'd pay the nanny for the same paid holidays you get at your own job.

Q. My mother has agreed to watch our daughter when I return to work. I don't like the idea of her working for nothing, though. It makes me feel that I can't tell her how I'd like things done. But she refuses to accept any payment. What else can I do?

A. Does she not want payment of any kind—or just cash? Some people feel strange about accepting money from family members. But they may be open to nonmonetary payment. My sister-in-law never paid my mother-in-law a dime for watching my four young nieces and nephews. But over the years, she furnished Mom with a new washer, dryer, and any other appliance that broke down. Another friend sent her sister/sitter (and husband) on a Caribbean cruise.

Q. Don't some companies offer a flexible benefits program that lets employees use some of those funds for child care? How does that work?

A. Many companies now offer what's called a Dependent Care Assistance Plan (or DCAP). Under this arrangement, you pay for child care out of your gross—not net—salary, which will save you a sizable amount in taxes come April 15. Here's how it works: You tell your employer how much money you want to put into the account for the coming year, up to a maximum of $5,000. (Every dollar you put into your account reduces your taxable income by one dollar.) That amount is then automatically deducted from your paycheck in equal installments. During the year, as you shell out money for the nanny, an after-school program, even summer day camp, you request a reimbursement from your account. The only drawback: You lose any money left in your account at year's end. If you're like most people, though, you'll find that child care costs, in the short term, are fairly predictable.

Q. My daughter will soon be attending a nearby family day care. I wasn't asked to sign anything. Should I draw up a contract myself?

A. Yes. But it needn't be a contract per se; a written agreement that outlines what you expect will suffice. Some points to include: Does the caregiver get paid weekly? By check, or cash? Under what circumstances are you expected to keep your child at home due to illness? Will you be expected to pay even if the child is out sick or on family vacation?

Q. Can I claim a tax credit for child care on my income tax?

A. Probably. You'll be asked to give your child care provider's name, address, and the amount you paid in child care on either Form 2441 (if you file Form 1040) or Schedule 2 (if you file Form 1040A). Most important, you have to supply the provider's taxpayer identification number (for individual providers, that's their Social Security number). You can't claim this credit unless you pay your sitter on the books. Otherwise, the IRS *will* catch you both. For more information on how much credit you're entitled to, see Chapter 11.

FOR MORE INFO

Child Care Aware offers a free brochure on choosing quality child care as well as tip sheets on how to find summer child care and before- and after-school care for children aged 5 to12: 2116 Campus Drive SE, Rochester, MN 55904; parent hot line, 800-424-2246.

National Association of Child Care Resource and Referral Agencies will give you the name and phone number of their local member agencies that can help you find child care alternatives in your area: 1319 F Street NW, Suite 810, Washington, DC 20004; 202-393-5501.

National Association for Family Day Care can give you a list of accredited family day care providers in your area: 206 Sixth Street, Suite 900, Des Moines, IA 50309-4018; 800-359-3817.

National Association for the Education of Young Children provides information on child care options: 1509 16th Street NW, Washington, DC 20036; 800-424-2460; www.naeyc.org/naeyc.

American Council of Nanny Schools offers a list of nanny schools that meet the Council's curriculum and training criteria: Delta College, University Center, MI 48710; 517-686-9417.

International Nanny Association provides a directory (for a fee) of its affiliated nanny agencies and nanny schools: 900 Haddon Avenue, Suite 438, Collingswood, NJ 08108; 609-858-0808; www.nanny.org.

NATIONAL AU PAIR PLACEMENT AGENCIES

For a complete list of authorized foreign au pair programs, contact the Exchange Visitor Program Services at the U.S. Information Agency, 301 Fourth Street SW, Room 734, Washington, DC 20547; 202-401-9810. A sampling of what's available:

Au Pair in America, 102 Greenwich Avenue, Greenwich, CT 06830; 800-727-2437.

Au Pair/Homestay, 1015 15th Street NW, Suite 1100, Washington, DC 20005; 202-408-5380.

Au Pair Care, One Post Street, Suite 700, San Francisco, CA 94104; 800-428-7247.

Au Pair Program USA, 6955 Union Park Center, Suite 360, Salt Lake City, UT 84047; 800-574-8889.

EF Au Pair, One Memorial Drive, Cambridge, MA 02142; 800-333-6056.

CHAPTER SIX

─────────■$■─────────

Living on One Salary

TO WORK, OR NOT TO WORK?

For Barbara Kays, the days started early—and ended late. At 5:30 every morning, she got up with her two preschoolers, showered and dressed in a suit ($175, plus $10 for dry cleaning), and whisked them off to the baby-sitter ($140 per week). She drove to her job ($4, round-trip) as budget manager and worked until noon when she grabbed a quick bite with a coworker ($8) before returning to work. At 5:30 she raced from the office to get the kids and pick up dinner: take-out rotisserie chicken and fixings ($15) because she often didn't have time to cook. She and her husband then bathed the children and read them a few stories. Once the kids were tucked into their freshly made beds ($35 for weekly housecleaning), Kays often worked until 11:00 P.M. on her home PC. At week's end, this 37-year-old asked herself again and again: Is it worth it?

The answer isn't clear. Nor is Kays's story all that unusual. Although more than half of all women with preschool children now hold paid jobs, many of them soon discover to their dismay that much of their earnings are eaten up by the costs of child care, a professional wardrobe, commuting, and other work-related expenses. Ultimately, some parents of young children discover that it's not worth it for both spouses to work. (See Figure 6.1.)

Obviously, each family's spending habits vary so widely, depending on factors from the type of child care they use to the kind of lifestyle that they lead, that it's almost impossible to generalize about how lucrative a second income actually is. And having the option to choose between working or staying at home with your child is a luxury that millions of single mothers and less affluent mothers can't afford. For women who are the primary support of their families, and for those whose husbands earn $30,000 or less, paid work is usually a necessity.

For many new mothers, however, the decision whether to work involves more than money. Even if you pay out in expenses almost as much as you earn, you may want to keep working anyway. Why?

- You love your job.

- Your job is an integral part of your identity.

- It will bother you to give up working for pay, or answering at a cocktail party that you're a stay-at-home mom.

- Talking to kids all day long will drive you nuts.

If you agreed with most of the above statements, working outside the home is probably critical to your happiness and satisfaction. (Ultimately that will affect your child's own happiness, too.) "Staying at home wasn't right for me," admits Gerry Greenwood Bournelis, the special events manager for the Children's Hospital Foundation in Milwaukee, Wisconsin. "I was almost depressed." Bournelis returned to work 13 months after she gave birth to her son (now aged

FIGURE 6.1   AT A GLANCE: THE COST OF WORKING

A hypothetical example below shows you how much you gain—or don't, depending on your viewpoint—when a married couple with a young child both work full-time. Also calculated is what happens when one parent stays at home. You can use this work sheet to crunch your own salary and expense numbers, but you can't simply copy these tax figures (even if you happen to make the same salary as our model couple). Taxes paid by a married couple will vary, depending on the state in which they live, the number of children they claim as deductions, property and mortgage taxes paid, and other itemized deductions. The numbers used below are based on a suburban married couple who live and work in Illinois. They have one child under age 3, a 30-year mortgage of $120,000 at 8%, and separate 401(k) plans. In their case, they gain an additional net cash flow available of only $2,162 when they both work.

He Works, She Works

Gross income:	
Husband	$65,000
Wife	$40,000
Total gross income	**$105,000**
Minus 10% annual 401(k) contributions:	
Husband	$6,500
Wife	$4,000
Adjusted gross income	**$94,500**
Minus taxes:	
Federal*	$13,530
State	$2,835
FICA	$8,033
Family's total take-home pay	**$70,102**
Minus additional costs of dual incomes†:	
Child care ($300 per week at a group day care center)	$15,000
Commuting	$1,150
Dry cleaning	$345
Lunches and coffee	$1,610
Take-out dinners	$2,000
Housecleaning	$1,200
Net income available for living expenses	**$48,797**

FIGURE 6.1 (CONTINUED)

One Works, One Stays Home

Gross income	$65,000
Minus 10% annual 401(k) contributions	$6,500
Adjusted gross income	$58,500
Minus taxes:	
Federal	$5,137
State	$1,755
FICA	$4,973
Family's total take-home pay	$46,635
Net income available for living expenses	$46,635

*Reflects a federal child care credit.
†Based on a 52-week year, minus 2 weeks of vacation.

Source: Hope Feinglass, CPA, CFP, Chicago, IL.

4). "I feel better about myself because of my job. And my son picks up on that," she says. "When I'm happy, I'm a better mom, a better wife, a better person."

What's more, even if you don't keep much of your earnings now, by continuing to work you're making a long-term investment in your career and future earnings. Child care costs, the heftiest expense by far for most working mothers, don't last forever. Eventually, that little tot will grow up and go to school. (Sure, you may still need someone to meet the school bus in the afternoon, but that'll cost you far less than full-time day care for a six-month-old.) And, by that time, most working moms will have probably gotten a raise, maybe even a promotion, and regularly siphoned some cash into a 401(k) or similar retirement fund. (See Figure 6.2.)

Building up a 401(k) nest egg—if that's an option for you

FIGURE 6.2   WHAT YOU LOSE LONG-TERM

Here's another look at our hypothetical working mom, showing what she stands to lose—in terms of salary increases and building up that 401(k) nest egg—if she drops out of the workforce for the next 5 to 15 years.

YEAR	SALARY*	401(K) BALANCE[†]
1	$40,000	$4,000
5	$43,602	$25,268
10	$59,843	$67,868
15	$97,026	$137,123
20	$167,870	$246,983

*Assumes a 4% increase per year.
[†]Balance at year-end, given a 10% contribution of salary per year and an annual return of 8%.

Source: Hope Feinglass, CPA, CFP, Chicago, IL.

at your job—may be a hidden benefit of remaining in the workforce, both in the short and long term. The 401(k) contributions give you an immediate tax break by reducing your current adjusted gross income. Every dollar you put in today will save you about 35 cents in federal taxes. Over the long haul, the money you sock away into a 401(k) grows tax-deferred. Obviously, the more you put in over the years—and the earlier in life that you do so—the larger your holdings will be upon retirement. And, if your employer matches all or part of your contribution, you're getting free money. That's akin to getting an annual, tax-deferred bonus, which you'd forfeit if you quit your job.

Meanwhile, women who step out of the paid workforce for an extended period of time may find that their earning power has diminished. Unless they go back to school or update their skills, these women may earn less than they did 5, 10, even 15 years ago when they stopped working to raise their kids.

Women who stay at home for years may even be putting themselves in financial jeopardy. These days, it's risky to depend on a single wage earner, given the constant threat of job layoffs. And divorce and widowhood—two real possibilities—often put nonworking wives in a precarious position if they forgo all responsibility for their financial future.

Of course, this whole does-it-pay-to-work scenario is somewhat lopsided. Isn't it rather sexist to assume that child care costs should be a woman's responsibility? Sort of. While child care is, in theory, a family expense (similar to your mortgage or electricity), that expense could be deleted from the budget if one parent stayed at home with the children. And that one parent is generally the mother. More sexism? Some husbands can and *do* stay home to raise the kids. But from a purely financial standpoint, it generally makes more sense for the wife to stay at home because women still earn less than men, on average.

The bottom line doesn't tell the whole story, though. For many mothers (and fathers), the decision whether to work boils down to parenting concerns, not money or career issues. Some parents don't believe in day care, or have found it impossible to find a loving, reliable, and affordable child care arrangement. "Do I really want someone else raising my child?" asks Denise Larkin. For this 33-year-old former international portfolio trader, the answer was no. Larkin quit shortly after the birth of her first child in 1996.

Other parents want to take a more active role in parenting; working long hours doesn't allow them to do that. "The time I spent with my children was always just too rushed.

And it was never the quality time that I had hoped for," explains Barbara Kays. "I had to put the brakes on." Ultimately, Kays quit her job. "As long as we keep our expenses down, we'll make it work," Kays says. Once the children attend school full-time, however, Kays plans to go back to work.

And round and round this argument goes. Unfortunately, what looks good on paper may not work out so neatly in real life. And what works perfectly for some parents and their kids may not work for you at all. Ultimately, it's a question only you can answer: Does this arrangement work for me and my family?

MANAGING ON ONE INCOME

You've decided that you're going to quit your job and stay at home to raise a family. Let's assume that you've already reconciled all the other issues discussed above, such as:

- What dropping out for a few years will mean to your career.
- The importance of retaining your financial independence.
- Whether you'll find it stimulating enough to be with the children all day.

The only question that concerns you now is: Can I afford to quit?

A lot of parents assume they need two incomes to survive. But, despite the popular image of mothers and fathers of young children both trooping off to work each day, it *is* possible to raise a family on one income. You'll have to do some careful planning first, though, if you're used to two paychecks and want to drop to one. Here's how to go about it:

DRAFT A NEW BUDGET

How much does your family need to survive? That's the point of this exercise. Base your new budget entirely on the take-home pay of the one spouse who's working, plus any extra income the other expects to earn (see "Get a Side Job" section later in this chapter). First, you need to figure out where your money goes. On a work sheet (see Figure 6.3), tally up your monthly expenses. (Most people find a monthly budget easiest to manage. For expenses that are billed annually, like insurance premiums, simply divide the amount by 12.) Create categories that work for you, and make those categories as specific as possible. Instead of lumping all of your food expenses together, for instance, divide them up into separate categories such as lunches out, dinners out, entertaining, groceries, and so on.

Include any debts such as a loan or the outstanding balance on a credit card. If you're expecting your first child, don't forget to budget for the baby: diapers, formula, clothes, and any large-ticket items like a carriage, crib, or car seat. (See Chapter 3 for more details on the costs of these items.)

After reviewing your one-paycheck budget, it may be clear that you *cannot* afford to quit. That's okay. You may still be able to make some less drastic changes. Spending more time with your kids doesn't necessarily mean that you have to stay home full-time. If half or even three-quarters of your salary will enable the family budget to be met, perhaps you can cut back your hours on the job. (For details about alternative work options, see Chapter 4.) Working four days per week instead of five could give you that extra quality time you want without strapping you for cash.

FIGURE 6.3   AT A GLANCE: TYPICAL FAMILY EXPENSES

ITEM	COST PER MONTH
Household	
Rent/mortgage, property taxes, and homeowner's insurance	

Utilities:
  Electricity
  Heat/fuel
  Telephone
  Water	

Groceries	
Laundry	
Gas/car repairs	
Personal	
Clothing	
Cosmetics	
Dinners out	
Subscriptions	
Books/videos/CDs	
Work	
Dry cleaning	
Transportation to work	
Lunches	
Children	
Formula	
Diapers	
Clothing	
Child care	
Allowances	

FIGURE 6.3 (CONTINUED)

ITEM	COST PER MONTH
Children (Continued)	
Lunch money	
Tuition	
Recreational programs	
Insurance	
Auto	
Disability	
Life	
Medical/dental	
Miscellaneous	
Gifts	
Pets	
Vacation	
Charitable contributions	
Debt Payments (Excluding Mortgage)	
Auto loan	
Personal loan	
Credit card balance	

CALCULATE THE COST OF WORK

Much of that second salary can get eaten up by obvious work-related expenses such as child care, commuting, and lunches. But there are some other hidden costs, too. Working full-time generally gives you less time for chores so you probably spend more money on household-cleaning services, car washes, yard maintenance, even minor household repairs. Your food bill may be higher, too, since you probably don't have the time or inclination to cook. Instead, you rely heavily on take-out and convenience foods.

Chances are you fuss more with your appearance when you go to the office, too. Add in those additional dollars spent on cosmetics, salon stylings, and clothes—a suit is pricier than jeans and a T-shirt. Maintenance of that clothing, such as dry cleaning, shoe repair, and alterations, will run you more, too. (To see how much your job costs you, fill out the work sheet in Figure 6.4.)

You won't kiss *all* of those work-related expenses goodbye, of course. Whether you work in an office or stay at

FIGURE 6.4   AT A GLANCE: HOW MUCH DOES YOUR JOB COST YOU?

CATEGORY	$ AMOUNT
A. Your gross earnings	
B. Your taxes and expenses:	
Federal income taxes	
State income taxes	
Social Security taxes	
Commuting	
Child care	
Business clothes	
Upkeep	
Cosmetics	
Lunches at work	
Convenience foods	
Total taxes and expenses	
C. Your real net income (subtract B from A)	

home, you still have to eat. Grabbing a bologna sandwich from the fridge is cheaper than the businessperson's lunch special downtown, of course, but you may find yourself eating lunch out frequently with the other stay-at-home moms and their tots. Even a quick chat over a cup of coffee and Danish will set you back a few bucks. Thinking of joining a play group? Gymboree, a 45-minute activity class for preschoolers, costs about $12 per session. What's more, you may find yourself doing more shopping now that you have the time. That's not altogether a bad thing, if you shop the sales. And your baby-sitter costs won't be eliminated entirely. You'll still need breaks away from the kids—to run errands or enjoy time by yourself.

CONSIDER THE COST OF TAXES

Families who drop from two paychecks to one obviously save the tax on the second income. Our hypothetical Illinois couple in Figure 6.1, for instance, save $8,393 in federal taxes, $1,080 in state taxes, and $3,060 in FICA taxes when they live on a single income of $65,000 compared to a combined income of $105,000.

TRIM THE FAT

To live on less, you have to spend less. That means you probably can't keep up your old lifestyle on just one salary. Are you doomed then to a life of tuna casseroles and thrift shops? Not really. You just have to be a bit smarter about your spending—and perhaps give up some of the luxuries.

Cutting expenses doesn't necessarily mean doing something drastic such as refinancing your mortgage or moving to a smaller house so that your mortgage payments would be lower; many families find that small cuts add up. For starters, pick a few expenses (from the categories you've created) that you can live without, or at least reduce. If you go out to the movies once a week, for instance, rent a video instead. Rather than grabbing take-out or ready-made foods, cook dinner at home more often. Consider swapping babysitting with another mom instead of paying for it. And, if you have an old car, repair it instead of financing a new one.

A three-week European vacation at five-star hotels will probably have to be postponed to the distant future. (Even if you could afford it, would you really take the kids on that kind of trip, anyway?) Car trips are cheaper, and more doable with kids in tow. If you can, camp out or stay with relatives or friends, which would be far cheaper than a hotel—and, for the kids, probably more of an adventure.

To make this cost cutting feel less like penny-pinching and more like the lifestyle choice that it is, both you and your spouse must agree that it's worth the sacrifice. Ultimately, you should feel that you're buying more time with your kids.

GET OUT OF DEBT

No one expects you to prepay your mortgage or car loan. But making the minimum payments on a credit card and carrying a high balance month after month (especially if you're paying a hefty interest rate of 18% or more) can strain even the best budgets when that second paycheck stops. Instead, use your savings—especially if it's sitting in a bank savings account earning just 3% in interest—to pay off those credit cards. If you own a home, you might think about consolidating your credit card balances through a home equity line of credit. You'll save on interest payments, because the interest rate for the consolidation loan should be substantially lower than the various rates you're now paying on your credit cards. (That's the reason most people get a consolidation loan.) In addition, the interest paid on credit card debt (and car loans, student loans, and other personal loans) is not tax-deductible, but the interest paid on a home equity line of credit *is*, on loans up to $100,000.

To make sure that you don't rack up those credit card bills again, adopt a pay-as-you-go spending style. If you can't afford to buy something with cash—or at least pay off your entire charge bill within three months—chances are you probably can't afford to pay for it with credit either. Most families can make do with one or two major credit cards. Having fewer cards on hand should reduce the temptation to spend, because you simply won't have as many credit lines available to abuse. To keep interest charges down, shop around for a bank card with lower interest rates. Bankcard Holders of America, a consumer-advocacy group, has compiled a list of banks with the lowest credit-card rates in the country. To get a copy, contact the group at: 524 Branch Drive, Salem, VA 24153; 540-389-5445.

Check Out Your Insurance

Families relying on a single paycheck need to protect that breadwinner's earning power with long-term disability insurance. Most companies offer their employees some type of coverage: either paid sick leave or actual disability payments in case you're unable to work for a long period of time. If your company doesn't offer such coverage, you can purchase your own individual policy—but you must hold a paid job to do so (a stay-at-home spouse can't get such a policy). Annual individual policy premiums range from $800 to $1,800. How much coverage do you need? Enough to provide between 60% and 70% of your gross income.

Both spouses, however, need adequate life insurance. Even though an at-home mom may not receive an actual salary, her care of the children and the home does have monetary value. If she were to die, her husband would have to pay hired help to fill her shoes. (How much life insurance do you need? See Chapter 12 for more information.)

Before leaving a job, a spouse should make sure that the family has adequate health insurance. If both spouses are covered under separate health plans at their jobs, can the stay-at-home spouse be added to the other parent's policy—and how much will it cost? On the other hand, if her husband has no coverage from his employer, a stay-at-home mom may have to continue the family's coverage through her former employer until other arrangements can be made. (For details, see Chapter 1.)

SET UP AN EMERGENCY CASH RESERVE

You should have three to six months of living expenses tucked away in a liquid investment such as a money market account. Think of it as your safety net should the breadwinning spouse suddenly be laid off or get sick. In addition, you won't have to turn to plastic for every unexpected bill.

If you don't have such a reserve already set up, build up those savings while you're both still working. The best way to do that: Pretend you've already stopped working. Cut back on the take-out dinners and other extras that you'll be giving up once one spouse stops working. That'll give you some idea if you can live on one income, and it'll help you stockpile the necessary savings.

GET A SIDE JOB

No matter how diligent a budgeter you are, you can always use more cash. That's why many stay-at-home types seek a sideline business that they can do in their spare moments. Some women sell cosmetics or Tupperware; others teach an occasional aerobics class; others work as a teacher's aide while their child is in school. Many market their professional skills, such as editing, selling, or accounting, on a consulting or freelance basis to a variety of employers. Still others start a home business—either building it from scratch or buying into a franchise. All of these side jobs are a way of keeping yourself out there in the work world while tending the home fires. And if you pursue these jobs vigorously, they could lead to lucrative second careers.

These days, the typical American works for more than 40 years. In the grand scheme of things, taking off five years or so to care for young children or to sample a second career doesn't necessarily have to spell a professional setback. It depends on how long you stay at home and what you do with your time while you're there.

QUESTIONS AND ANSWERS

Q. Am I cheating my kids if I go back to work rather than stay at home?

A. Unfortunately, no one can answer that question but you. If you're working so many hours that you generally leave before the children wake up each morning and arrive home after they're tucked into bed at night, you probably should reevaluate your priorities. But, if you work a reasonable schedule that permits you to spend chunks of time with your little ones, if they're in a quality child care arrangement when you're not around, and if you like and enjoy your job, everyone may actually benefit from the situation. Don't overlook the fact that the money you earn may go toward building a better life—be it a college fund for the kids or the down payment on a house—for your family.

Q. As a new mother, I really want to stay at home. How do I avoid feeling like a dropout compared to all my still-working friends?

A. As corny as this sounds, you have to know in your heart that this is the right thing to do. Working moms and stay-at-home moms continue to denigrate each other because, by doing so, they can justify their own position. (A few years ago, a magazine actually dubbed this growing tension "the mommy wars.") Hopefully, your close friends will understand—or at least tolerate—your decision. The others? Better brace yourself for rude questions like "But what do you do all day?" and "Aren't you a feminist anymore?" Ultimately, both working and stay-at-home moms struggle with the same issue: Am I doing the right thing for my family and myself?

Q. I'm confused about this tax issue. If I bring home a paycheck, too, will our family be pushed into a higher tax bracket?

A. Here's how it works: In computing taxes for a married couple, the federal government collects 15% of the first $40,000 of taxable income (that's the amount the couple has to pay taxes on after subtracting personal exemptions and deductions); 28% of everything between $40,000 and $97,000; and, in most circumstances, 31% or more of everything above that. Let's say, for example, that a husband's taxable income is $30,000 and his wife takes a job earning $20,000. The family will pay 15% on the first $40,000, but will pay 28 percent on any amount above that (in this case, on $10,000).

Q. We're expecting our first child next month. I would like to stay at home for at least the first year, but I'm not sure we can afford it. That "baby gear" expense keeps throwing our new budget off balance. Any suggestions on how to cut back?

A. Most parents buy their first child quality, top-of-the-line stuff, even if they can't afford it or if a cheaper version will do. How come? Nothing is too good for your child. But you can make do on far less, and baby will never know the difference.

Take clothes, for example. In the first two years, most children outgrow their togs before they wear them out. (My kids wore some outfits only once.) And, since couples are having just one or two children these days, baby clothes don't get passed down and worn out. So rather than running up a hefty clothing tab, ask friends or relatives for hand-me-downs, or shop garage sales. You can usually pick up a barely worn snowsuit at one of these local sales for just three bucks (compare that to $50 at a store).

FOR MORE INFO

Still confused about how to make it all work? These books might help:

Staying Home: From Full-Time Professional to Full-Time Parent, by Darcie Sanders and Martha M. Bullen. $10.95; 1992, Little, Brown. Order department: 200 West Street, Waltham, MA 02154; 800-343-9204 (except in Massachusetts); 800-759-0190 (for Massachusetts residents); 781-890-0875 (fax).

Two Incomes and Still Broke?, by Linda Kelley. $20.00; 1996, Times Books, a division of Random House. Order department: 400 Hahn Road, Westminster, MD 21157; 800-733-3000.

The Tightwad Gazette: Promoting Thrift as a Viable Alternative Lifestyle, by Amy Dacyzyn. $12.99 each; Vol. 1, 1993; Vol. 2, 1995; Vol. 3, 1997; Villard Books, a division of Random House. Order department: 400 Hahn Road, Westminster, MD 21157; 800-733-3000.

CHAPTER SEVEN

The Grade School Years

Your six-year-old just barreled down the block on his two-wheeler—sans the training wheels. Your nine-year-old spent the night at her first slumber party yesterday. And for the past half hour, your 12-year-old has been chatting on the Internet with some kid who lives halfway across the country. Your children, those helpless little neophytes who once did little more than eat and sleep, are blossoming into full-fledged people.

Unfortunately, as your youngsters grow, so does the cost of maintaining them. Grade-schoolers eat more than babies. Often, they wear out their clothes before they outgrow them. It'll cost you more to entertain them, too, especially if they develop a passion for sports or music, or both. While Junior used to be happy to simply hang out with you and bang some pots and pans in the kitchen, now he needs a computer, a racing bike, and a complete collection of Yankee baseball cards, just like his best friend next door has. Welcome to the middle years, ages 6 through 12.

Let's start with the good news: The day your child hops on that bus to kindergarten, your child care costs should drop dramatically. Your medical expenses should nosedive, too, since kids of this age are usually well past the frequent ear-infection stage. (And those hefty orthodontist and dermatologist bills generally don't come until adolescence.) In addition, your family's income has likely increased since the little bambino first arrived, due to cost-of-living increases, merit raises, and/or promotions. You or your spouse may even be returning to full-time, paid employment.

Don't get too excited, though. While those fixed expenses may drop, your so-called discretionary spending will probably mushroom. After-school activities like piano and tennis lessons—as well as summer camp and more elaborate family vacations—take a bigger bite out of your budget during this period. Schooling may require additional funds if the local public schools are not well run or if you want your kids to receive a certain kind of education. You may have a gifted child who needs the enriched curriculum and individualized attention of a private school, for instance, or a slow learner who needs a completely different environment.

Deciding where to spend your discretionary dollars won't be easy. You'll have to make trade-offs now in a way you haven't done before. Should you buy the bigger house with the less than perfect school district, or the smaller house with the enviable one? Will you go to Disney World this year, or buy a baby grand piano for your budding Van Cliburn?

What's more, that college tuition, which once loomed so far in the distance, is fast approaching. Financial experts insist that you must start saving for college as soon as you give birth. (How to fund your child's college education is discussed at length in Chapters 9 and 10.) But, honestly, it's very hard to sock away that extra cash, especially when you have a lot of other expenses like child care that must be met *now*. Many parents simply assume that they'll speed up their savings later on, when they have more discretionary funds at their disposal. Unfortunately, *now* is that time.

So . . . while you probably will find yourself with lower child care and medical costs and more cash on hand when your child enters elementary school, you'll have several new voices clamoring for that money. Get ready to make some tough financial choices.

KARATE, BALLET, SOCCER—AND THOSE DREADED PIANO LESSONS

When I was growing up in New York City in the late 1960s, after-school activities meant playing jump rope or stickball with the other kids on the block. Today, most kids play soccer, T-ball, or some other organized sport—as well as attend beginner's classes for ballet, tae kwon do, and swimming— before they're six years old.

How much can you expect *this* to cost you? Plenty. Gone are the days of shelling out just 95 bucks for 10 weeks of Gymboree. Prices will vary, of course, depending on where you live and what type of activity your child is enrolled in, but here's a sampling: Karate lessons for a seven-year-old boy at Karate for Kids in Salt Lake City cost $1,020 for the year. Private swimming instruction for a six-year-old at Saf-T-Swim in East Meadow, New York, costs $169 for six half-hour sessions. And ballet lessons for a five-year-old dancer at the Ballet Center in Charlottesville, Virginia, cost $128 for a once-per-week, 16-week program.

The good news is that some of these expenses are going to be short-lived. Kids, especially younger ones, are like that. This week, karate is all the rage; two months hence they won't be able to live without tap dancing lessons. If your child really clicks with a program, however, it's apt to run you far less now than it will in seven years or so. By the time your Dorothy Hamill wanna-be hits her teens, for example, she'll presumably have advanced to the level where she needs (1) more expensive equipment, such as several pairs of custom-made ice skates as well as workout clothes and elaborate costumes for performances; (2) private lessons; (3) several weeks of skating camp; (4) ballet lessons to perfect her on-ice gracefulness; (5) entrant's fees and other charges if she participates in a local or state championship; and (6) tickets to see a touring ice show so that she can watch professional skaters in action.

Ultimately, how much you spend on karate, cello, or Swahili lessons depends on how much cash you have free, and what your motivations are. It's a bit harder to budget for these expenses than it was for, say, formula and diapers during the early years, because these lessons aren't absolutely *needed*. (Yes, they will enrich your child's life, but they're not essential to survival.) And the money—and time—spent pursuing one activity can't then be used to simultaneously pursue another. You and your child have to decide whether ice skating rather than the flute or sculpture is worth the required funds and commitment.

If you think that giving little Clara piano lessons at age 3 will earn her a trip to Carnegie Hall eventually, forget it. That's about as likely to happen as winning the lottery. But if she's really interested in music, piano lessons will broaden her horizons and may enhance her socially. Joining a school orchestra or band is a way to make friends, for instance. And those music lessons may well teach her something more than just how to play the piano. After many hours of tedious practice, she'll hopefully find that she can master a skill—if she sticks with it. That's a good lesson for anyone to take into adulthood.

To hold expenses in check, you should try to keep the investment low, at least initially. Remember that kids are fickle. This week, it's the violin; next week, it'll be the flute. Your public school may be able to help you out here. Some school music programs offer group lessons. Some even provide instruments on long-term loan. This is a sensible outlay for a budding interest. If your child is really enthusiastic (and shows a modicum of talent), this type of lesson won't suffice forever. But it's an efficient and affordable way to assess if playing the drums is a real interest or just another flight of fancy. My own sense, too, is that you're more likely to hear a realistic assessment of Junior's skills from the school's program. Private teachers may exaggerate his capabilities a bit to win him as a long-term student.

If your school doesn't offer any such program, contact a local college. The music department should be able to recommend a graduate student who's preparing for a career as a music teacher (and who will, presumably, charge less than a typical instructor). Some other money-saving tips? Start with a simple, inexpensive instrument. My son's school starts with the recorder. It's easy for beginners to master, and a plastic, student-sized recorder costs just five bucks. (A sturdier wooden model will run you about $20.) If your child insists on a costlier instrument, rent one instead. Or, buy a secondhand instrument through the classified ads. (There must be at least one poor parent out there who is trying to unload a clarinet bought prematurely when a child insisted on taking lessons. Two months later the clarinet was relegated to the linen closet because the child decided to play football instead.) Finally, you can sometimes save money on lessons by paying the entire fee up front, or by enrolling more than one child at the same time.

Like lessons, organized sports programs vary widely in price, depending on the particular sport and your child's age and level of proficiency. Often, these deals are a relative bargain (again, at least during the early years). My son's soccer league, for instance, costs about $60 for the fall and spring seasons. That includes a registration fee and a team uniform. (Parents are responsible for buying cleats and a size 3 soccer ball, which set me back about $25.) Were I to sign his younger brother up too, it would cost an additional $40, plus $25 for shoes and a ball. Each season is 10 weeks long: there's one after-school practice and an hour-long game on the weekend. That's a lot of activity for just $60. Keep in mind, however, that my son is just six years old and soccer is a relatively inexpensive sport. Ice fees and equipment for kids his age who play hockey, for instance, cost $150 or more.

If my son continues to play soccer—and is good at it—I expect the price tag to jump dramatically. He'll need higher-quality spikes, shin guards, balls, and so on. He'll probably want to go to soccer camp for at least one week during the summer. And if he makes the state championships, my husband and I and our two other kids will have to drive to Albany to watch the match, which will involve staying at a hotel and eating out because it's a five-hour drive from our home on Long Island. And that's only one sport. He's just informed me that he wants to play baseball and basketball next year, too.

SUMMER CAMP

Just when you thought you were free of child care worries, along comes summer and those 10 school-free weeks. What's a poor parent to do? For many, the answer is summer camp.

Obviously, camp isn't just a convenient drop-off for your kids during the dog days of summer. It's a place where kids hone new (and old) skills, make friends, and learn to be independent. Spending time away from home and parents is, after all, an important part of growing up. And the leisurely, noncompetitive camp environment encourages many children to explore interests that they might not (or could not) otherwise pursue at home or in the classroom.

Generally, summer camps fall into two categories: day camps and resident (or sleep-away) camps. Day camps operate on a daily basis. Campers return home every evening after a half-day, three-quarter-day, or full-day session. The season lasts for one week to two months. These camps, which cater to children from nursery school age to teenagers, are usually coed, but campers are often grouped according to sex and age.

Resident camps, on the other hand, give kids the chance to sample life away from home in a group setting. For many children, going away to camp is the first significant time they spend away from their families. Like day camps, the season lasts from one to eight weeks. Camps can be single-sex or coed, and the campers' ages range from 8 to 15 years old. Because of increasing pressure by dual-income families, some camps now accept resident campers as young as six, but many still do not.

Sleep-away programs can be general-purpose or specialized. General-purpose camps involve a range of outdoor and indoor activities such as competitive sports, swimming, nature study, arts and crafts, and hiking. Specialized camps cover some of the same ground but concentrate primarily on a sport such as soccer, a talent such as music or theater, or an interest such as space. Some sports camps offer a 7- or 14-day program, called a clinic, which has both day camp and resident options. Many specialty camps focus on self-improvement: There are weight loss camps, computer programming camps, even oceanography camps. And several cater to special-needs children such as those with diabetes or the hearing-impaired.

None of this splendid enrichment for your child is free, naturally. Fees at a private, all-purpose resident camp run about $40 to $120 per day, according to the American Camping Association. Camps run by not-for-profit groups, however, like the Boy Scouts or the YMCA, range from $15 to $85 per day. (Generally, the camper must attend a private sleep-over camp for at least four weeks, a nonprofit camp for at least two weeks.) Most day camps—both nonprofit and private—charge $10 to $50 per day.

In addition to regular tuition, camps often charge extra fees for certain programs and activities such as horseback riding or off-site trips. You'll also need to pay for round-trip transportation and fork over some spending money. Most require some basic equipment like a sleeping bag, flashlight, and rain poncho that could add a hundred dollars or so to your tab. In general, the more expensive the camp's tuition, the more you can expect to pay for extras. (See Figure 7.1.)

Like any other expenditure, you have to shop around to get your money's worth. Find out what your child wants and is capable of doing. All-purpose camps can't nurture a talent like a specialty camp can. If you have a budding

FIGURE 7.1 AT A GLANCE: THE COST OF SUMMER CAMP

ITEM	YOUR COST
Tuition	
Extra fees	
Equipment	
Transportation	
Spending money	
Total	

ballerina on your hands, it may be worth the extra money to send her to Belvoir Terrace in Massachusetts or Camp Encore Coda in Maine. Day camp, on the other hand, is much cheaper than sleep-away camp and may work better for younger kids or children who are anxious about being away from home.

Camps run by not-for-profit groups generally cost less, but you get less for your money, too. The meals and accommodations aren't as top-drawer as their more expensive counterparts. Does that matter to you? Does that matter to your child? Some camps also offer partial or full scholarships. The Girl Scouts and Boy Scouts of America, for instance, offer "camperships." To find out about the availability of such aid—and any eligibility requirements—you'll have to check with these organizations and/or the camps themselves.

There are some 8,500 day and sleep-over camps in the United States to choose from. Finding the right camp ultimately takes time and effort. Your best bet is a personal referral. Talk to your friends and have your children do the same. Those who've had previous experience at a particular camp can give you the lowdown on what it's really like. Don't just ask others if they liked a particular camp, though. Ask them *what* they liked—and didn't like—about it. In addition, you should check the following sources for information about other camps in your area:

- *Attend a camp fair.* Camp directors set up information booths—complete with videotape demonstrations—to hawk their camps. Generally, these fairs are held off-season at schools. Contact your nearest American Camping Association office (800-428-CAMP) to find out about upcoming fairs in your area.

- *Use a referral service.* Staffers ask you what you're looking for (i.e., your child's age, type of camp you want, and your price range) and then try to find a camp that meets those needs. Some regional offices of the American Camping Association offer this as a free service. Many private referral agencies do it for free, too. Generally, they pass the cost along to the camp in which they eventually place your child. (In that case, the agency charges the camp a percentage of the tuition fee for each child placed at the camp.) But some referral agencies may charge you a flat fee for their service. To avoid confusion, ask in advance about fees for all placement services.

- *Check out the camp directories.* The annual guide of the American Camping Association, the only official accrediting organization, lists all camps that live up to the group's 300 health, safety, and program-quality standards. You'll also find tips on choosing the right camp and comparing costs. Look for *The Guide to ACA-Accredited Camps*, American Camping Association, 5000 State Road 67 North, Martinsville, IN 46151; 800-428-CAMP; www.aca-camps.org.

- *Get brochures from several camps.* Obviously, the camp itself isn't exactly an objective source. Its pamphlets all picture happy, smiling children. But the brochures do give basic information that you need to make an intelligent decision: the price, the ages of kids who attend, and the activities available.

- *Arrange a tour or visit.* Many camps invite families to visit their facilities, during both the off-season and when camp is in session. Be sure to talk to the camp director, who sets the tone for the whole operation. Ask if the director has a background in education, or is simply an entrepreneur. Does he or she take a hands-on role in running the place, or operate as an absentee owner? (For more sample questions, see the accompanying box.)

QUESTIONS TO ASK A CAMP DIRECTOR

- What's the program like? Is it highly structured, or do campers have some free time to pursue their own interests? Are any of the activities compulsory? Do the activities emphasize competitiveness or cooperation? If it's a specialized camp, are lessons given in a group or individually?

- What's the staff like? What are the qualifications of instructors and counselors? What percentage of staffers return each year? What's the ratio of campers to counselors—especially for water and other higher-risk activities?

- Is there adequate medical supervision? Is there a doctor or nurse on staff at all times? Are the counselors trained in first aid or CPR? Where is the nearest hospital?

- What's the program's track record? How long has the camp been in operation? Is it accredited by the American Camping Association?

- How are disciplinary problems handled? What are the camp's rules of conduct, and how are violations—both big and small—handled?

- Do you provide family references? (Most camps can supply names and phone numbers of satisfied parents and kids who will talk with prospective parents. If they can't, that may be a sign to look elsewhere.)

- Who are the other campers? (To feel at home, your child should be in camp with at least some children of his or her own age.)

- How do children stay in touch with their families? (Policies vary from camp to camp, but most programs expect kids and their parents to stay in touch mostly through letters. Certain days are set aside for family visits. Ask how homesickness is handled, especially if this is your child's first experience away from home.)

- What's the payment schedule? (At most camps you must pay the tuition in full before camp begins.) What happens if a child leaves before the end of the summer? Does the camp offer refunds? What about extra fees for off-site trips, equipment, and other activities? How much spending money does a child generally need?

PUBLIC OR PRIVATE SCHOOL?

Every child in the United States is entitled to a free education at the local public school. But for many grade-schoolers (and their parents), that just won't do. Perhaps your
public school no longer offers what your youngster needs,
such as an enriched curriculum for gifted students, because of government cutbacks. Or, your child has a learning difficulty, which is not being addressed by the school's
teachers. Maybe you simply want your child to attend a
school that reinforces your religious values. (Because of the
constitutional separation of church and state, our public
schools obviously can't do that.) So you start thinking
about private school.

Many private schools are affiliated with a church or some
religious organization, such as a parochial school or a
yeshiva, and attract students of the same religion. But your
child doesn't necessarily have to be a member of that religion to attend. You might want little Jane to go there just because the school has such high academic standards.

Some private schools meet the needs of "special" children: kids who suffer from mental retardation or those who
have behavioral or emotional problems. These institutions
may offer therapy as well as special education to blind, deaf,
or brain-damaged kids. Other schools, such as military academies, may instill discipline. Still another type of private
school caters to students who are intellectually or artistically
gifted. Here the budding artist, ballet dancer, or musician
can pursue individual interests while being schooled in traditional course work.

How much will such a school cost you? Prices vary widely.
Choate Rosemary Hall, a prep school in Wallingford, Connecticut, costs $23,715 per year for boarders and $16,720
for day students. Eagle Hill School in Hardwick, Massachu-

setts, which is designed for kids with learning disabilities, costs $33,500 per year for boarders and $20,600 for day students. And Oak Ridge Military Academy in Oak Ridge, North Carolina, costs $12,380 per year for boarders and $6,825 for day students.

Before you fork over that tuition, however, keep three things in mind: (1) If you own a home, you pay taxes to support your local schools; (2) you're essentially throwing those tax dollars down the drain if your kids don't attend the public schools that you support; and (3) the money spent on a private school education during the grade school years is money you could be either spending to enrich your child's life in other ways now (e.g., skiing in Vail every winter) or saving to fund that Ivy League college education later on. (If you're set on sending the little one to private school, then skip this section. But many parents sometimes feel that they have no other choice, when, indeed, they do.)

Public schools are funded largely by local taxes, which you, as a homeowner, must pay. Some communities can't—or won't—spend the necessary dollars to provide a top-notch school. Education funding varies widely, therefore, not just by state but by community within the state. It's not uncommon, in fact, for schools in adjacent neighborhoods—the schools could literally be located within a mile or two of each other—to have completely different academic records. One may send a large percentage of its students to college; the other may have a high dropout rate.

What can you, as a parent and a taxpayer, do about ensuring that your local public school is a school you'd want to send your kids to? First, make it a priority when you a purchase a home. According to the National Association of Realtors, a good school district is one of the four primary reasons why people decide on a home. (The other three are price, neighborhood, and commuting distance from work.) Even buyers without children ask about school districts because they know it'll be an issue when they sell their home.

Of course, you'll pay more for good schools. In Saratoga, California, for instance, home buyers pay close to $50,000 more for a house in the better of the two school districts. In Winchester, Massachusetts, a small town eight miles north of Boston, buyers pay $332,000, on average, for their homes—and solid-gold school district. Buyers in the neighboring town of Arlington, however, pay $223,000, on average, for their homes and a school district with a lesser reputation. In Ohio, Michael Bond, an associate professor of finance at Cleveland State University, found that when comparing school districts, every percentage-point increase in the students' overall passing rate of the state's high school proficiency test meant a $300 increase in the price of a home. Passing rates ranged from 90% in the Cleveland suburbs to 15% in the city itself, which could mean as much as a $22,500 difference in price.

Most home buyers are forced to make a trade-off: Do you buy the house that's both bigger and more affordable, but the school district is shaky, or do you settle for a home that's probably smaller, a bit pricier, but has a highly regarded school district? You'll have to do some calculating here. In some cases, it may make more financial sense to buy the less expensive home in the questionable school district than a costlier house with a high tax bill and better schools. Why? The money that you save on the house's purchase price and lower property taxes could be enough to send your student to private school. But the savings would have to be considerable, especially if you have more than one child.

If you already own a home and have just learned that

MAKING THE GRADE

What makes one school district better than another? Your real estate agent may throw several different statistics your way: SAT scores, graduation rates, percentage of graduates who go to four-year and two-year colleges, per-pupil spending, average class sizes, and student/teacher ratios. But this data is often outdated and can be misleading, if you don't understand what the numbers represent. Some people address the class size question with talk about the student/teacher ratio, for instance. But that's meaningless if schools include secretaries and administrators—all their personnel basically—in their student/teacher ratio; that figure won't tell you how many kids are in Mrs. Johnson's chemistry lab, either. Other parents focus on Scholastic Assessment Test (SAT) scores as an indicator of a high school's quality. But the SAT measures innate ability more than what is taught in school. (Some critics say that the SAT favors kids of a certain socioeconomic level, but that's another story.)

For a more accurate picture, look at per-student expenditures. This figure alone won't tell you if school funds are being spent wisely, but it will give you some idea of how well the school can provide for each student. You should also look at some test scores. For an elementary school, check out the math and reading scores for the district's fourth graders. (Almost every state keeps these statistics, along with similar scores for eighth and tenth graders.) You can get this information directly from the school. For high schools, review the achievement test scores. They'll tell you what a student has learned about a particular subject like math or history. Advanced Placement (AP) test results will tell you if the honors courses are good. Of course, any test data can be fudged or manipulated, so don't make a judgment about a school based solely on these scores.

When picking a school, you must take into account your child's potential. Will your student do well in a highly competitive school? Or would he or she do better in a smaller school with a warmer atmosphere? If you can, visit the school and sit in on a few classes. (Not all schools let you do this, however. And you certainly can't do it without making arrangements in advance.)

Often, the public schools in a university town and the more affluent suburbs are better than those of the surrounding neighborhoods. University faculty members and (presumably) more educated, professional parents are concerned with the quality of the education their children receive. They're willing to pay taxes to support it.

your school district is less than exemplary, you could try to send your kids to a better public school in a neighboring town. Not all schools accept outsiders, but some do. You may be charged an annual fee of $1,000 to $4,000. (In most cases, that's still far less than a private school tuition.) You'll also have to make your own arrangements for transportation; the school bus won't pick up an out-of-towner.

If the problem is simply that your child is advanced and needs more stimulation, you should see about enrollment in a gifted program. (Again, if your school doesn't offer this, a neighboring one may.) Perhaps your child could skip a grade. Or, you could try to supplement public education yourself with vacations to interesting locales, after-school computer classes, a specialized summer camp that focuses on particular talents, or private ballet lessons rather than group instruction. All of these alternatives will cost far less than a private school education.

Your last alternative may be to move to a town that offers a better school district. That's no easy feat, especially with kids in tow, but over the long run it could save you thousands of dollars in tuition fees.

QUESTIONS AND ANSWERS

Q. I never took piano lessons as a child, but now, as an adult, I wish that I had. I'd like my daughter to begin lessons in the fall, but she doesn't seem enthusiastic about the idea. Should I sign her up anyway?

A. Lessons of any kind are likely to be most successful when a child asks about them spontaneously, or else responds positively when you suggest it. Don't push it. Lessons that are forced on a youngster to make up for what the parent didn't have as a child rarely come to anything.

Q. If the property taxes are higher in one community than another, does that mean it has better public schools?

A. Not necessarily. High taxes don't guarantee good schools. In fact, if there are a large number of businesses in a community, they'll pay the lion's share of the taxes. Because of that business tax subsidy, residents may pay low taxes and have better schools.

Q. My 10-year-old is going to sleep-away camp for the first time this summer. What happens if he gets hurt in an accident or becomes ill?

A. The staff should be well trained in health and safety issues. A good camp will have an infirmary and at least one nurse on the premises, as well as a working relationship with a hospital and a doctor on call at all times. There should be a policy in place (probably explained in the camp catalog) that states at what point a parent is notified about a child's accident or sickness. (If no mention is made of this, ask the camp director.) Also, ask about the camp's health and liability coverage in these types of situations.

FOR MORE INFO

For the inside scoop on the schools in your area, try these two sources:

SchoolMatch (5027 Pine Creek Drive, Westerville, OH 43081; 800-SCHOOL-1; www.schoolmatch.com) publishes school "report cards" that compare your school district with other schools across the country.

National School Reporting Services (2001 West Main Street, Suite 175, Stamford, CT 06902; 800-229-4992; 800-229-4992; www.theschoolreport.com) puts out an even more comprehensive book that lets you compare one district to another.

To get the lowdown on summer camps, try these two camp directories:

Peterson's Summer Opportunities for Kids and Teenagers ($26.95; Peterson's, P.O. Box 2123, Princeton, NJ 08543-2123; 800-338-3282; www.petersons.com).

Choosing the Right Camp: The Complete Guide to the Best Summer Camp for Your Child, by Richard C. Kennedy and Michael Kimball (latest edition is from 1995; no longer available through the publisher, Times Books, but you should be able to find it at the library).

For a list of private schools, check out these two books:

Peterson's Private Secondary Schools 1998–99 ($29.95; Peterson's, P.O. Box 2123, Princeton, NJ 08543-2123; 800-338-3282; www.petersons.com).

The Handbook of Private Schools ($90; Porter Sargent Publishers, 11 Beacon Street, Suite 1400, Boston, MA 02108; 617-523-1670).

CHAPTER EIGHT

$

The Teen Years

This is it, folks. You're in the final stretch before college. The apple of your eye just became a *teenager*. Brace yourself for some outrageous fashions, some rebellious behavior—and some extra expenses.

According to U.S. Department of Agriculture figures for a family with an average before-tax income of $46,100, your 12- to 14-year-old costs $730 more each year now than he or she did up to this point. (And you thought diapers and formula were expensive!) Between the ages of 15 and 17, the cost rises an additional $130. How come? Clothing costs more. Kids are now approaching grown-up sizes and will wear only the very latest fashions. (Forget about those hand-me-downs or end-of-the-season bargains you used to scoop up.) They also eat more—especially the guys. For lunch, a 16-year-old boy will think nothing of gobbling up a Big Mac, large fries, and a shake ($6.13) at McDonald's. Two hours later, he'll be ready for another such "snack."

What's more, your teenager will soon be driving. Even if you don't plan on buying him or her a car, you'll still have to add the new driver to your auto insurance policy, which can raise your premiums by 50% to 70% (and, in many cases, even more) each year. Medical costs may be on the upswing again, if your adolescent needs braces, counseling, or acne treatment. But the biggest budget-buster may be the parties: the coming-of-age events such as a bar mitzvah, a high school graduation, even a Sweet 16 birthday, which can cost almost as much as a wedding.

Your one saving grace may be that teenagers can get after-school jobs or earn some pocket money baby-sitting or mowing lawns. At the very least, this should help offset the added adolescent expenses. But it probably won't do much to stave off the typical parent-teen conflict: They need money to buy compact disks, faddish clothing, junk food—and all you can think about right now is saving every cent for their college education.

THE ALLOWANCE ISSUE

You've probably been giving your kids an allowance for years. What better way to teach them the value of a dollar, right? But the pocket change you've been doling out so that they could buy a small toy or that extra candy bar won't cut it during the teen years. Kids over 12 want more: more money to buy more clothes, more concert tickets, more mascara, more everything. Generally, they can handle a bit more financial responsibility, too.

How big an allowance you give will depend on how much you can afford, the age of the child, and, to some extent, the going rate among other teens in the neighborhood. A good rule of thumb: Don't give so much that your youngster can freely buy everything he or she wants, or so little that there is just enough to cover a few of the basic expenses.

With a teenager—as with any age child—you need to set

some ground rules first. How will the allowance be spent? In many households, the parents pay for necessities; the kids pay for optional items or luxuries. While a seven-year-old is likely to spend the entire dole on comics, a teen will probably stock up on sneakers or styling mousse. Decide ahead of time if any purchases, such as junk food, will be off-limits. Whatever guidelines you establish, though, be clear; then let your child alone. If money is squandered on ear-splitting CDs, so be it. After all, an allowance is money kids are *allowed* to spend. (You can ask them to turn the music down, however.)

Ideally, as your child moves through the teen years, the allowance should cover as many expenses as possible—clothing, compact disks, in-line skates, bus fare, school field trips, school lunches, movie tickets, lunch at McDonald's, and so on. (You'll have to adjust the amount accordingly.) This will give hands-on experience with the saving, spending—and yes, wasting—of money. What's more, it could help defuse many a potentially explosive parent-teen confrontation. Mom and Dad can't be expected to pick up the tab for yet another leather jacket if 16-year-old Susie pays for her own clothes with her allowance money.

Some parents dock their children's allowance if they neglect to do chores. Others withhold payment if a report card isn't up to par. But those tactics not only risk defeating the purpose, which is to teach kids how to manage money, but they may actually send the wrong message—often leading children to associate money with love and acceptance.

An allowance and chores are really two separate issues. Most child care experts agree that children should learn to take out the garbage, mow the lawn, or do other household chores because they're part of a family unit, not because they are paid to do so. If children fail to do assigned chores, parents can restrict other privileges, such as watching a favorite TV program. If you want to teach your teen about earning extra money by working for it, let her earn bonus bucks by doing extra chores, such as cleaning out the garage or raking the leaves in the fall.

SLINGING BURGERS, BUSING TABLES, AND OTHER AFTER-SCHOOL JOBS

Nothing short of living on their own will force kids to learn about money management faster than earning actual wages. Whether they're flipping burgers, busing tables, or operating a paper route, a paying job helps instill a good work ethic. It also teaches teens about courtesy, responsibility, and time management.

When kids earn their own money, they understand for the first time how much things cost. They may be less inclined to fritter away $75 on a designer jacket, for example, if it takes them a week to earn that cash mopping floors at the local Dairy Queen. That new racing bike may mean more to them, too, if they save up their earnings to buy it. And, while the money earned at an after-school job can't provide enough funds for a college education, it could help defray the cost somewhat. In some cases it could mean the difference between attending a state college and a private college.

But doesn't manning the checkout line at the local supermarket detract from a teen's primary job—getting an education? Most educators agree that spending too much time on an outside job can hinder a student's academic performance. Working up to 20 hours per week, however, is quite manageable—and usually beneficial for most teens. The most recent study of 29,000 11th graders by the Educational Testing Service found, in fact, that students who worked up to 20 hours each week had higher grade-point averages than those who didn't work at all. Students with jobs also watched far less television.

The real question, it seems to me, is not whether your teenager should get a job, but rather: What will be done with the money earned? If an entire paycheck is frittered away on fad clothing, junk food, and other extras, then it's questionable what is actually gotten out of the experience. Wouldn't it be more beneficial to spend these formative years playing soccer or studying judo rather than working for minimum wage to simply buy more *things*? Spending so much just to keep up with the Joneses will give any teen an unreal picture of the world. (And we parents know far too well that teenagers are already in desperate need of a reality check, especially when it comes to finances.) In grown-up life, after all, a huge chunk of one's paycheck must cover necessities like rent and food—not luxuries.

If your young person is using the money productively, however—to save for a car, college education, or some other big-ticket item, let's say—then working at an after-school job may well prove to be a valuable lesson in saving and earning money. What's more, it could help you, as parents, balance that family budget a bit more easily.

IT'S PARTY TIME

At first, it was just a clown or some kid's dad dressed up like Barney. Then it was a pony and cart and a goody bag stuffed with homemade chocolates. This year it was a petting zoo, a magician, and a hot dog vendor on the front lawn. (Each guest took home a goldfish.) How can any rational parent hope to compete with—never mind afford—such a celebration? It isn't easy. But this is what's expected on the party circuit today, often starting with a child's first birthday.

You don't have to fall prey to this extravagance, of course, especially for a child's birthday. You could throw a birthday bash for the big years: 13, 16, and 18. Or, you might throw a nice party every other year. On the "off" years, let a few close friends be invited over for a sleep-over or a Saturday afternoon at the movies. You could always do something different like pack a picnic lunch and take a handful of kids to a children's museum, the zoo, or the aquarium. (It's far cheaper than one of those party packages for 20 kids at the local amusement park or laser tag arena.)

No matter how frugally you manage these birthday parties, though, you'll probably find yourself splurging for the coming-of-age events: the bar/bas mitzvahs, the confirmations, the graduations (junior high and high school), and, ultimately, the bridal showers, engagement parties, and weddings. (Indeed, all of these fetes may well rival a wedding in complexity and price.)

A bas mitzvah, for instance, could set you back nearly $15,000, if you want a sit-down dinner for 100 guests on a Saturday night, complete with cocktail hour, flowers, a deejay, and photographer. A buffet for those same 100 folks at the local VFW hall, where you bring the food, soda and cocktails, decorations, and the deejay, costs about $2,000.

How much should you spend, and how do you budget for such an expense? That depends on how much money you have, and what kind of party you want to throw. Plan ahead as much as possible. How many guests will you invite? Will the celebration be held at your home? Will it be catered? If you hold the party at a catering hall, will it be a sit-down dinner or simply a cocktail party? Will you need a photographer, floral arrangements, and/or a deejay or a band? Price each item out at today's prices (just to get a general idea of the cost involved), and then start putting some money away in a separate account.

If you can't save for these events, don't be tempted to go into debt when the time comes. (That means no loans, no cash advances, and no credit cards.) Either use the funds you have available or, if you're strapped for cash, scale back a bit. The kids probably won't care all that much. If they do, explain your financial situation and get them involved. Ask them how *they* think you could pull the party off with the money you have. (You'll be amazed at the results. Teens, for instance, care more about good music and dancing at a party than food. So they'll probably tell you to nix the dinner and just serve hors d'oeuvres. Or they may think that balloons will do instead of flowers.)

Should you decide ultimately that your eldest only graduates from high school once so you're going to pull out all the stops (and blow your budget), keep in mind that children have long memories. You threw a $5,000 bash aboard a cruise ship for son Jimmy's high school graduation? Daughter Emily will expect nothing less when her turn comes.

BRACES, A NOSE JOB, AND OTHER ELECTIVE MEDICAL EXPENSES

During the teen years, medical costs should be lower. Childhood illnesses are ancient history, and the teens are the healthiest years in the life cycle. But you may find yourself shelling out big bucks for *elective* medical expenses that aren't necessarily covered by your insurance plan. With adolescence, unfortunately, can come bills from the orthodontist, the dermatologist, the plastic surgeon, and/or the psychologist.

This is a somewhat gray area, budgetwise. Should you go into debt for these expenses? How much planning and saving should you do in advance? That depends. You'll have to clearly distinguish between "want" and "need" in these situations. Let's say that your daughter could use braces. Does she need them to correct a serious problem? Or do you just want her somewhat crooked teeth to look model-perfect? Similarly, private sessions with a psychologist may be necessary for your 15-year-old if you and your spouse have a messy divorce. But it may be a bit of a luxury if your son is merely suffering from the normal teenage angst.

The trouble is you probably won't know in advance what you need. You can't predict that an eight-year-old child will have terrible acne, for instance, at 16. (Obviously, if you needed braces as a teen, there's a strong possibility that your child will, too.) The best remedy is to sock some cash into a separate account, if you can. Call it "unexpected expenses" or a "contingency fund."

Just how big a bite will these elective expenses take out of your budget? Orthodontia is often not covered by dental insurance, so you may have to pay a good chunk of the bill out-of-pocket. The cost of a typical set of upper and lower braces to correct crooked teeth and a bite problem runs about $3,600. Often, you must pay one-third up front; one-third halfway through treatment; one-third at completion. (Expect the braces to be worn for at least three years.) A nighttime retainer to hold the teeth in place after the braces are removed, meanwhile, will run you another $250 or so.

Rhinoplasty (or a nose job) is rarely covered by medical insurance, either, unless it's needed to repair disfigurement that resulted from an accident. A simple nose job will run you about $3,000. The patient will be sidelined with nasal packs, a splint, and some swelling for one to three weeks. To have the chin reconstructed too, so that it flows better with the new profile, that's another $1,300 to $2,000. And should your daughter want to complete the picture with a pair of full lips, collagen implants cost about $300 per injection.

You may fare better financially with the dermatologist. Most insurers will cover treatment for your teen's poison ivy rash or latest bout of acne as well as removal of a wart or mole. Dermatologists generally charge an initial consultation fee of $100 or so. Each follow-up visit runs $75 to $85. Treatment varies, obviously, depending upon the severity of the condition, but the average acne patient will see the doctor every four to six weeks for a full year.

Health insurance companies often cover the costs of emotional illness, too. A 50-minute individual session with a psychologist in private practice could run you from $85 to $150. An hour-and-a-half group therapy session will cost far less—as little as $50 per visit, in many cases—and the "group" effect may actually help your teen see that he or she is not alone. Some of the issues troubling your teen are no doubt the very same issues that teens all over are grappling with. Unfortunately, insurers are more apt to cover individual sessions than the group variety. Family therapy may be another less costly alternative over the long haul. When everyone works together, this type of therapy generally gets to the root of the problem quicker than individual therapy.

One way to save on all of these elective medical expenses is to take advantage of a *flexible spending account,* if it's offered by your employer. According to a 1997 survey by Hewitt Associates, a consulting firm that specializes in employee benefits, 85% of employers currently offer a health care or dependent care spending account. Here's how it works: You estimate your family's annual out-of-pocket health care expenses, up to a maximum amount set by your employer. Your employer deducts the money from your salary—pretax— and deposits it into a special account. You can then draw on that money to pay for medical expenses like orthodontia and psychological counseling—even deductibles and copayment amounts—that are not covered by your health insurance plan. The savings can really add up. If you put $1,000 into the account, you'd save roughly $300 in taxes (depending on your income level and tax bracket). The only drawback? At year's end, you lose whatever money is still left in your account. You cannot roll that money over to the following year. Still, you might come out ahead anyway. According to that same Hewitt survey, the median amount left in such health care accounts by most people was just $100. Let's assume that you've put $1,000 into an account (and thereby saved $300 in taxes). Even if you leave 100 bucks in the account at year-end, you'll still have saved $200. (How? The $300 tax savings minus the $100 left in the account.)

QUESTIONS AND ANSWERS

Q. At what age should I begin giving my son an allowance?

A. I'd start giving him a weekly allowance at age five or six. It's hard for kids to understand the concept any earlier than that. You might begin by giving the allowance on a special day, such as your child's birthday. Lay some ground rules: Tell him that he's old enough now to have money of his own. Ask him what he thinks he'd like to buy. Then tell him what you expect him to buy with his money—candy or a small toy, perhaps. Finally, explain that his allowance should last through the week, and that you want him to put any left-over money into a piggy bank. That way, if he runs short one week, he can borrow from himself.

Q. My 16-year-old just got an after-school job at our local supermarket. Since she's now earning a salary, should I stop giving her an allowance?

A. That depends on what you expect her to do with her money. If she's allowed to spend both her allowance and her salary as she wishes, I'd decrease the allowance. You don't want kids to have so much money on hand that they can afford whatever they desire. They'll never learn anything about the value of money. But if you expect your daughter to bank her earnings for college or a large purchase, like a car, I'd still give her an allowance to use as spending money.

Q. This year I gave my daughter a clothing allowance and let her shop on her own. She came home with the worst wardrobe I've ever seen. What should I do?

A. You made the deal, so you have to stick with it—ugly clothes and all. I wouldn't ask her to return anything, unless they're inappropriate. She shouldn't wear a see-through blouse to school, for example, or pants that are too tight. Ditto if she didn't buy the basics like underwear and socks but spent her whole clothing budget on a leather jacket and boots. Next time, you might help her draw up a shopping list before she makes her purchases.

Q. I'm ready to cave in. Every time I want to use the phone, my teenage daughter or son is using it. How much will it cost me to get a separate line for the kids?

A. Prices vary across the country. In New York City, for example, a second phone line and additional phone jack will cost you $202—plus about $12 per month for standard service from Bell Atlantic. A telephone will run you about $30.

Q. My 17-year-old plays football on his high school team. If he's injured, will he be covered by my medical insurance plan?

A. Medical costs that arise from athletic injuries of minor, dependent children are generally covered by the parents' health insurance plans. The one exception: Dental work is usually not covered. You could always bring a suit against the school to recover nonreimbursed dental costs, but you must prove that the school was either negligent or didn't provide prompt and competent medical care. Just the fact that your son was injured is not enough to win a lawsuit.

FOR MORE INFO

Piggy Bank to Credit Card: Teach Your Child the Financial Facts of Life, by Linda Barbanel (Crown, 1994, $10; 800-793-2665) explains what money means to children at each age. It addresses "the gimmes," allowances, saving, even shoplifting.

The *Young Americans Bank* offers services solely to kids 21 years old and under, nationwide. Savings accounts may be opened by mail. Kids can also apply for credit cards. Contact them at: 311 Steele Street, Denver, CO 80206; 303-321-2265.

CHAPTER NINE

College-Bound

Y ou've been through the birth, the Barbies, the bicycles, the braces, even the bar or bas mitzvah. But you still have to face the single most pressing financial issue for parents: how to pay for college.

It's a doozy, folks. For many parents, the cost of a college education costs more than any other family purchase, except a house. At some elite schools, for instance, the price of a four-year education has already cracked the $100,000 mark. How will you ever save such an amount? Where should you invest your money? And, most importantly, when and how should you get started? This chapter attempts to answer those questions, or at the very least, give you enough information so that you can begin to formulate your own college savings plan.

HOW MUCH?

How much depends on the school you choose. Most state colleges and universities are a relative bargain, especially for in-state students. But if you want to send your young person to a pricey Ivy League college starting in the year 2000, for instance, a four-year tab will run you about $150,000. A good private college, meanwhile, will cost you about one-half to two-thirds of that sticker price. And a good public college or university in your state is even less: about one-third of the cost of Harvard and its ilk.

For over a decade, both public and private college costs increased annually by 8% or more, well above the inflation rate. But in recent years, tuition hikes have slowed to about 5%. This trend is expected to continue for the next several years, thanks to schools' increased cost-cutting efforts and a bigger college-age population.

You'll likely need at least $50,000. If you have two children, you'll need twice that much. (See Figure 9.1.) And that's not the whole story. The college tab will include more than just tuition and room and board. Students also need books and supplies (a computer is almost a necessity); equipment if they play tennis or the flute; clothing; and money for recreation, laundry, haircuts, and telephone calls. What's more, they'll want to come home for holidays and/or vacations so will need either a car—and, then, money for gas, upkeep, and insurance—or plane, train, or bus fare. Expect to shell out several thousand dollars per year for these additional items. (See Figure 9.2.)

Of course, you may not have to foot the entire bill yourself. Your family may qualify for some financial aid and/or grants and other scholarships. (See Chapter 10 for more details on financial aid.) But you'll probably have to finance some of it. Even with maximum financial aid, most people can expect to shell out up to $10,000 per year for a private college, or up to $4,000 for a public college. Financial aid simply doesn't cover everything. It's meant to fill in the gap, not give a student a free ride. In fact, most financial aid packages—even those for the neediest students—include loans and/or a work-study job.

FIGURE 9.1   AT A GLANCE: COLLEGE COST WORK SHEET

Before you begin your college savings plan, you'll need to estimate how much college will cost for your child. While it's impossible to accurately predict future inflation rates or the future price of college tuition and fees, the following work sheet should give you some idea of how much money you'll need.

1. Child's current age

2. Years until college (subtract Line 1 from 18)

3. Annual college cost (use current amount, or: public—$8,720; private—$19,242)

4. Future annual college cost (multiply Line 3 by rising cost factor from table below)

5. Number of years of college planned

6. Total cost of college (multiply Line 4 by Line 5)

Rising Cost Factor

YEARS TO COLLEGE	MULTIPLY LINE 3 BY*
1	1.08
2	1.17
3	1.26
4	1.36
5	1.47
6	1.59
7	1.71
8	1.85
9	2.00
10	2.16
11	2.33
12	2.52
13	2.72

FIGURE 9.1 (CONTINUED)

Rising Cost Factor (Continued)	
YEARS TO COLLEGE	MULTIPLY LINE 4 BY*
14	2.94
15	3.17
16	3.43
17	3.70
18	4.00

*The figures assume an 8% yield compounded annually.

Source: Reprinted with permission from Mutual Fund Education Alliance, Kansas City, MO.

SAVE WHAT YOU CAN

So . . . how are you going to come up with all this money? You have to cut back on your spending. You have to save. And you have to invest wisely.

Some people get so discouraged by the staggering cost of college tuition that they never even try to save to meet those costs. It's just too hard. Others try to amass 100% of the tuition—and quit a few years into their savings program because they can't reach their goal. Neither plan works. You should sock away *something* for your youngster's college education, but the truth is, most parents can't—and don't—save the entire amount. A more realistic plan? Try to save at least half of the estimated tab before Joe College heads off for campus. And assume that some combination of current income, loans, student jobs, scholarships, and financial aid will make up the rest. (See Figure 9.3.)

For many families, that strategy still may be easier said than done. The key is to start somewhere, even if you can

**FIGURE 9.2 AT A GLANCE: TUITION, ROOM
AND BOARD—AND EVERYTHING ELSE**

EXPENSE	FIRST SEMESTER	SECOND SEMESTER
Tuition		
Dorm housing *or* off-campus rent		
On- *or* off-campus meals		
Books		
Supplies		
Equipment		
Computer		
Clothing		
Laundry		
Prescriptions and other medical costs		
Haircuts and other grooming		
Entertainment		
Telephone		
Recreation		
Travel to and from school		
Miscellaneous		
Total expenses		

only scrape together $50 a month. Any amount of savings is better than none. And the sooner you start saving, the better. Remember: Time does amazing things for money. If you put away $1,000 this year and give it 18 years to grow with a return of 8%, for example, it will be worth $4,000 when Junior goes away to college.

FIGURE 9.3   AT A GLANCE: SOURCES OF FUNDS FOR COLLEGE

Savings and investments. Don't try to save the entire tuition bill. It's overwhelming for most families. Instead, aim for 50% to 75% of the projected cost. Start saving as soon as possible.

Your current income. You'll probably have to dig into your own pockets. But chances are you'll have more discretionary income now that your kids are older.

Student jobs. Your kids can work during vacations and/or part-time when school is in session. Work-study programs let students earn some of their tuition by working at a job.

Grants. Free money that's given to students based on need. Unfortunately, most middle-class parents don't qualify.

Scholarships. More free money that isn't necessarily need-based. Many schools offer awards to students who are gifted in academics, athletics, or the arts.

Loans. Student and personal loans are a common way to get needed cash, but, obviously, this is the most costly source. Young college graduates just starting out will be saddled with loan repayments for years; otherwise you'll have to assume the debt, just when you're probably thinking about retirement.

It would be nice to assume that you'll put a certain amount away each month or year and take advantage of dollar cost averaging. (When you regularly invest a fixed amount in a stock or mutual fund—no matter if the market goes up or down—your average purchase price is lower than the average market price over the same time period. That's dollar cost averaging.) But things may not work out as planned. Some years you may have to spend extra for remedial tutoring or braces; other years you may earn a bigger bonus at work or a larger refund from the IRS. The key, again, is to put some amount away. If you can do it regularly, fine. If not, a fits-and-starts program may prove just as effective over the long term.

Of course, saving money is only half the battle. While most savings and investment accounts will help your money grow over the years, some investments are better suited to your needs than others. If you trust your savings to investments that are too conservative, for instance, you run the risk that your investments won't keep up with inflation and taxes. Plunk those dollars into a vehicle that's too risky, and you could lose it all. Your savings should be invested so they reap the biggest return (assuming an acceptable amount of risk) within the time frame you have.

Your Investment Strategy

Whether you invest in stocks, bonds, or certificates of deposit depends a lot on your personality and your willingness to tolerate risk. As an investor, you must always balance the safety and security offered by a conservative investment like a money market account with the greater growth potential offered by a riskier investment such as a stock.

When should you go for growth, though, and when should you stick with something more secure? That depends on how much time you have to invest your money. When selecting an investment for a college fund, your strategy will be influenced by the age of your college-bound child. The general rule is that the closer your child is to attending college, the more conservative your investment should be. Timing is an important factor in any investment plan. If you need the funds earmarked for college in two or three years, you can't afford as much investment risk as you might have 10 years earlier. That means most of you will have to alter your college fund investment strategy as you go along.

INFANCY THROUGH AGE 12

Now's the time to think lo-o-o-o-ong term. Since you have so much time until your child starts college, you can afford to take some risks. Pick an aggressive investment like growth stocks or a no-load mutual fund that invests in growth stocks. Contribute regularly and leave your money there, even if the market takes a dip. You have time to ride the ups and downs of market cycles. Stocks have consistently delivered the best returns on your money in the long run. Over the next 10, 12, or 15 years, your funds should outperform bonds, Treasury bills, and money market accounts by a significant margin. To be avoided, however: high-risk investments like the commodities market and limited partnerships.

Sample portfolio:

80% stock funds

10% bond funds

10% money market funds or certificates of deposit

THE TEEN YEARS

The trouble with stocks, of course, is that they can fall in price. Sometimes it takes several years to recoup your losses. And if Junior will be attending college in a few years, you may not be able to wait for the market to turn around. You need the money *now* to pay those tuition bills.

That's why, when your youngster reaches high school age, you should start easing your money out of stocks and into shorter-term, more conservative investments that pay a fixed rate of interest. Basically, you need to start thinking like a short-term investor. With college just a few years off, it's too risky to have so much money invested in stocks. But don't get too conservative. Forget those savings accounts.

(For the interest you'd earn, you might as well just stick the money under your mattress.) Instead, consider short-term bonds or certificates of deposit. Just before college payments start, switch enough cash to a money market fund so you can write checks against it. Within two to three years of that first tuition bill, your college fund (or at least the funds needed for freshman year) should be out of stocks entirely.

Sample portfolio:

0–60% stock funds

40% bond funds

0–60% money market funds or certificates of deposit

DIVERSIFY

Investing for your child's college education is like investing for any other long-term goal. Some alternatives are better than others, and diversity is the key to happiness. Even if you plan on putting most of your money into a particular kind of investment—stock mutual funds, let's say—it's best not to put all of your money into the same fund. If you can, spread your money—and, thus, your risk—among three stock mutual funds. That way, should one fund underperform, the other funds will help cushion your loss.

Here's the scoop on a few of the most popular savings options for college:

STOCKS

Over the long haul, nothing outperforms stocks. For most of us, it's better to invest in a stock (or equity) mutual fund rather than individual stocks, because funds offer diversification and professional management to both large and small investors. You can invest $2,000 in a mutual fund, for instance, and reap the same rate of return as someone who invests $20,000. Your risk is reduced, too, because the mutual fund's assets are invested not in just one stock, but in many different stocks.

Most funds require a minimum investment of $1,500 to $2,000, but many waive that requirement if you sign up to have money automatically transferred from your checking account to the fund every month, or you set up either a UTMA or UGMA account. (See Chapter 13 for an explanation of these accounts.) When shopping for a mutual fund, choose a no-load fund with a good performance record.

BONDS

When a company, the government, or a municipality issues a bond, it is basically writing an IOU to raise money. You lend money to the issuer by making an investment in a bond and are repaid, with a fixed rate of interest, when the bond matures at a later date. Some investors think bonds are a good, stable college investment because you know exactly how much your investment will be worth when the bond matures. If you need $30,000 in 15 years, for example, then you must buy enough bonds today that will pay that amount upon maturity. What's more, the longer the maturity of the bond, the lower the price you'll initially pay because there's more time for the interest to build up the value of the bond.

The trouble with bonds, though, is that unless you hold them until maturity you risk losing some of your principal. Bonds have an inverse relationship with interest rates. If interest rates have risen since your bond was issued, for instance, your bond is worth less than it was worth when you bought it. If interest rates have fallen, your bond is worth more. None of this makes any difference, of course, if you plan to hold your bond until maturity. But it makes a big difference if you want to sell ahead of time. So . . . if you want to include bonds as part of your college fund, make sure that you buy bonds that will mature when you're paying tuition—not three years later.

You've probably heard about a number of different types of bonds. *Series EE savings bonds* are fully insured U.S. government bonds, which you buy for half their face value. (A $100 bond costs $50.) While the returns aren't spectacular on these bonds (5.59% currently), you pay no tax on the accumulated interest until the bonds mature and you cash them in. An added bonus: If you bought them after 1989—in your name, not your child's—and use them to pay your child's college tuition, all of the interest you earn on those savings bonds will be tax-free. There are restrictions, of course. To qualify, your adjusted gross income (including the interest earned on the bonds) cannot exceed certain limits set by the IRS. You can buy series EE bonds from commercial and savings banks and, possibly, your employer.

Like savings bonds, *zero-coupon Treasury bonds* are sold at substantially less than their face value and don't pay any interest until they mature. A $1,000 bond may sell for $500 and be redeemed 10 years later for the full value. (Your effective interest rate: 7.10%.) What troubles some investors about this product is that, although you don't receive any money until the bond matures, you must pay tax on the interest earned each year as though you had actually received it. Essentially, you're paying tax on money you never got. (It's often referred to as the "phantom tax.") You can buy zero-coupon bonds from securities firms, discount brokers, and local banks.

Baccalaureate bonds are a type of municipal bond sold by some states especially for college savings. They come in maturities ranging from 5 to 21 years. Their main attraction is that they're exempt from federal income tax—and state and local taxes, too, if you live in the state issuing the bond. As with other bonds, buy a baccalaureate bond that will mature when you need it. If you have to cash in early, you could take a loss.

CERTIFICATES OF DEPOSIT

With a *certificate of deposit*, you deposit a set amount of money—often $500 or more—and you're guaranteed a stated interest rate at the end of the period. (CDs come in a range of maturities: 1, 2, 3, 6, and 12 months; 2 years to 10 years.) Their interest rates generally don't keep pace with other investment options—CDs with a two-year maturity will pay about 6% in 1999—and you'll usually pay a penalty for early withdrawal. Often, CDs may be good investments for college savings that you'll need in a few years.

The College Savings Bank of Princeton, New Jersey, offers a special CD called the CollegeSure CD designed just for college saving. The variable interest rate matches the college inflation rate—currently, 4.62%. Each CD is sold in units or fractions of units. (Upon maturity, one full unit, for example, is equal to one full year's cost for tuition, fees, room and board at the average four-year private college.) You buy enough units to cover your child's college costs when the time comes. If your child decides not to go to college when the CD matures, you can get your investment back, plus interest. For additional information on the program, contact the College Savings Bank, 5 Vaughn Drive, Princeton, NJ 08540; 800-888-2723.

ARE PREPAID TUITION PLANS WORTH IT?

You can pay for your child's college tuition now even though he or she won't step foot on campus for another 18 years. Prepaid college tuition plans, which let you lock in tomorrow's cost at today's price, are growing in popularity. Florida, Michigan, and Wyoming created the first state-sponsored programs 10 years ago. Today, more than a dozen states offer them, and others are preparing to roll their own programs out soon. Are they worth it?

That depends. Very conservative investors might like these plans because basically they're buying a sure thing. A couple contributes money to the plan while their child is young. In return, the state guarantees to cover all or a portion of the tuition costs (depending on how much you contribute) when your kid enters a state college or university years later. Other investments, obviously, can't offer such a guarantee. But most other investments, such as a stock mutual fund, would certainly earn a better yield than any of these plans.

Earnings grow tax-deferred and are taxed (at the student's rate) when the money is withdrawn to use for college. In addition, new federal law now allows the plan to cover not only the expenses of tuition, books, and supplies, but room and board as well. Still, what happens if Junior decides he doesn't want to go to Penn State—or to any local college at all? Some plans allow the use of funds at out-of-state and even private colleges, but you'll probably have to fork over some more dough. Public colleges may charge you higher nonresident rates, and private schools, well, they just cost more than a state college. If Junior decides to skip college altogether, you'll generally get back what you contributed but with no interest added.

Still, some families—especially lower-income families—might find these plans appealing because the minimum investment amount is usually lower than that required by most mutual funds. Most plans also let you invest annually or monthly; other features, such as payroll deduction and automatic transfer from a checking or savings account, make it easy to set aside money regularly.

SOME COLLEGE TAX BREAKS AND OTHER MONEY-SAVING TIPS

Thanks to the Taxpayer Relief Act of 1997, some families may now get a break from Uncle Sam to help pay for the cost of a college education. As of 1998, taxpayers (students or their parents) can deduct the interest paid on qualified education loans for the first 60 months of loan payments. The deduction limit is $1,000 in annual interest paid in 1998 or later (even on loans taken out before 1998); by 2001, the limit rises to $2,500 per year. This deduction, however, begins to phase out for married couples (filing jointly) who have an adjusted gross income of more than $60,000. (For single filers, it's $40,000.) The deduction disappears entirely if you earn $75,000 jointly ($55,000 for singles).

Starting in 1998, families may also take advantage of two new tax credits for college spending. The *Hope Scholarship* lets a family take a tax credit of up to $1,500 each year for each student in the family. The credit is allowed for tuition and related expenses (but not room and board) for the first two years of college. After that, the *Lifetime Learning* credit kicks in. This credit is worth 20% annually of the first $5,000 spent on college expenses through 2002 for each student (i.e., up to $1,000); after 2002, the credit jumps to 20% of the first $10,000 in expenses (i.e., up to $2,000). Both credits begin phasing out for married taxpayers (filing jointly) who have adjusted gross incomes of $80,000 or more. (For single filers, it's $40,000.)

Another new offering is the *Education IRA*. Families can contribute up to $500 per year, per child, to an education savings account, starting in 1998. Who qualifies? Families with adjusted gross incomes of less than $150,000. (For single taxpayers, it's $95,000 or less.) Although your contributions are not tax-deductible, the earnings are free if the money is used for education expenses. All contributions must be made before your child turns 18, and you must use the funds before he or she is 30. Otherwise, the beneficiary pays income tax on the earnings, plus a 10% penalty on the balance. Money unused in one account may be rolled over into another child's Education IRA. One caution: You can't take tax-free withdrawals from this IRA the same year you use the Hope or Lifetime tax credit. And contributions can't be made in the same year that you make state prepaid tuition plan payments.

In addition to Uncle Sam's generosity, you can shave even more money off that college tab, if you know where to look. First, consider a school near home. That could save you a bundle. If your child can live at home and commute, you'll save on room and board expenses. Plus, many states offer residents with good grades and a certain family income (it varies by state) financial incentives to attend local state colleges. Have your daughter spend the first two years at a junior college (the tuition is less), before transferring to a four-year school for the last two years. (Check in advance that all course credits are transferrable.) Perhaps your son would like to attend the same college as an older sibling. A few colleges and universities offer tuition discounts for the second member of the family who enrolls. Finally, encourage them to take those Advanced

Placement (AP) courses in high school. Many colleges give credit for these. If students take enough AP courses in high school, they might be able to cut out a semester or two at the university. That'll cut your four-year tab by up to one-fourth.

QUESTIONS AND ANSWERS

Q. Can I use the money in my regular IRA to pay for my son's college tuition, or must I open one of these special Education IRAs?

A. As of 1998, if you're younger than $59\frac{1}{2}$, you can withdraw from a regular tax-deductible IRA to help pay for college without having to pay the 10% early withdrawal penalty. (If you're older than $59\frac{1}{2}$, of course, you could always withdraw the money for any purpose without incurring the penalty.) Whenever you make a withdrawal, however, you must pay income taxes on that money, whereas with an Education IRA you don't pay any tax on your money even when you take it out, as long as you use the funds to finance Junior's college education.

Q. My wife and I have just started saving for our son's education. Should we put the money in his name, or ours?

A. Your name, probably. Since the "Kiddie Tax" became effective in 1987, sheltering money under your child's name doesn't save you as much in taxes as it once did, unless you're in the top tax bracket. Then you may want to put the money in Junior's name. (For a more detailed explanation, see Chapter 11.)

But if getting financial aid is of primary concern, keep the funds in your name. When it comes to calculating the amount of aid a student will receive, the student is expected to kick in a larger share of his or her own assets (35%) than you, the parent, are of your own savings (5% to 6%). That means a student with few assets will hit the 35% threshold sooner—and thus qualify for financial aid sooner—than the student with a big savings account.

Finally, when you put money in a child's name—either directly or through a trust or custodial account—you're basically giving up control of that money. At 18, your child may decide to use the money for college as you planned—or may opt to take an extended vacation in Bora Bora instead.

Q. We started our family late in life (my husband and I are both 40) so our two kids will be entering college just when we're thinking about retiring. Should we invest whatever money we have for college tuition, or our own retirement?

A. Save as much as you can for retirement, instead of for their college tuition. Why? First, colleges generally don't include your retirement account as an asset when figuring your child's financial aid package, so you may qualify for more aid than if you had set up a separate mutual fund for their education. Second, if you tap into that 401(k) when you're actually retired, those earnings may be taxed at a lower rate than the rate you were paying during your working years.

Q. I've often heard people talking about buying a cash value life insurance policy for their child as a way to save for college. Is this a good idea?

A. Generally, no. Kids don't need a life insurance policy of their own because they don't contribute to the family's income. And that's what life insurance is for. (See Chapter 12 for more details.) Despite what insurance company projections might tell you, a cash value policy as an investment generally won't deliver the kind of returns you need to build up a sizable college fund. The only people who would benefit from such a savings plan, I suppose, are parents who need the forced-savings feature of such a plan. In all other cases, you can probably do better investing your money elsewhere.

FOR MORE INFO

To get the most recent interest rate on your Series EE savings bond, call 800-US-BONDS.

Contact the *College Board* about Advanced Placement exams and courses available to high school students: 45 Columbus Avenue, New York, NY 10023; 212-713-8177; www.collegeboard.org.

CHAPTER TEN

Finding College Financial Aid

I t's just about this time that parents become discouraged: I should've saved *more* money. I should've worked *more* overtime. Clipped *more* coupons. Shopped *more* thrift shops. Hindsight is always best. Now you have to worry about sending Junior to college, and you don't have enough money to foot the bill. Meeting the high cost of a college education is a struggle for all of us. (Yes, wealthy folks can afford it, but they're not reading this book.) If you've socked a good chunk away, fine. Chances are, though, you still need some extra cash to make up the gap between the cost of schooling and what you've saved over the years. And that means you have to apply for financial aid and/or take out a loan.

What kind of aid is available, and how much can you get? There are three basic types of aid: grants, loans, and scholarships. The federal government, state governments, private lenders, foundations, clubs, organizations, and the colleges themselves offer a variety of deals. Most service clubs such as Rotary International and the Elks, for instance, offer scholarships. State governments frequently award grants to resident students attending state schools. (Some give them to out-of-state students, too.) And the federal government offers low-interest-rate loans to both students and their parents.

The amount of financial aid you get is determined by something called *financial need.* And the government has its own rather complicated formula for figuring this out. Here's how it works, roughly: First, the cost of the education is assessed. From that figure is subtracted your "expected family contribution," which is determined largely by your income but also by other factors such as your assets and the number of kids you have in college at the same time. The amount that remains is your family's "financial need." (See Figure 10.1.) This information is then sent to the various government agencies and to your selected colleges, who will then conduct their own needs analysis.

To apply for federal student aid grants or loans, you must fill out the Free Application for Federal Student Aid (FAFSA). There is no fee. Many state agencies and universities also use this form to award their own funds. But many colleges, especially the private ones, make you fill out a second form, the Financial Aid Form (FAF). Expect to pay a processing fee for this form based on the number of colleges that will receive the information. Both forms are available from any high school guidance office or college financial aid office.

Some loan programs, however, require you to apply directly to a lending institution, such as a bank, credit union, or savings and loan association. At many colleges,

FIGURE 10.1 AT A GLANCE: CALCULATING YOUR FINANCIAL NEED

The Simple View
What it costs to attend college (tuition, room and board)
– Your expected family contribution (looks at income, assets, and other variables)
= Your financial need

Work Sheet: Approximate Expected Family Contribution for 1998–1999
The following chart will give you a ballpark estimate of how much you'll be expected to pay for your child's college education (based on the standard "financial need" analysis system) in 1998–1999:
1. Your Adjusted Gross Income for 1997: (If your child earned more than $2,500 in 1997, include 50% of the amount over $2,500 in the income figure.)
2. Your Assets: Include your home. (That's the current real estate value minus the unpaid balance on your mortgage.) Cash, savings, stocks, etc. (If your child has savings, add 35% of that amount to the savings figure.) Total Assets
3. Family Size: (Include you and your spouse, the student, and other dependent children.)
4. Your Approximate Family Contribution: (To determine this amount for one child in college, match the figures you've listed on lines 1, 2, and 3 with the figures in the chart on pages 180–181.)
5. Adjusted Family Contribution: (If more than one family member will be in college at least half-time during the same year, divide the family contribution on line 4 by the number in college.)

FIGURE 10.1 (CONTINUED)

ASSETS		$20,000	30,000	40,000	50,000	60,000	70,000	80,000	90,000	100,000
					INCOME BEFORE TAXES					
$20,000										
FAMILY SIZE	3	$800	2,700	4,400	6,800	9,500	12,600	15,600	18,500	21,400
	4	0	2,000	2,600	4,700	8,200	11,400	14,300	17,200	20,200
	5	0	900	1,900	3,700	7,000	10,200	13,100	16,000	19,000
	6	0	0	1,200	2,800	5,800	8,800	11,800	14,700	17,600
$30,000										
FAMILY SIZE	3	$800	2,700	3,400	5,800	9,500	12,600	15,600	18,500	21,400
	4	0	2,000	2,600	4,700	8,200	11,400	14,300	17,200	20,200
	5	0	900	1,900	3,700	7,000	10,200	13,100	16,000	19,000
	6	0	0	1,200	2,800	5,800	8,800	11,800	14,700	17,600
$40,000										
FAMILY SIZE	3	$800	2,700	3,400	5,800	9,500	12,600	15,600	18,500	21,400
	4	0	2,000	2,600	4,700	8,200	11,400	14,300	17,200	20,200
	5	0	900	1,900	3,700	7,000	10,200	13,100	16,000	19,000
	6	0	0	1,200	2,800	5,800	8,800	11,800	14,700	17,600
$50,000										
FAMILY SIZE	3	$1,000	2,900	4,300	7,300	10,100	13,600	16,100	19,100	22,000
	4	400	2,300	3,500	6,200	8,800	11,900	14,900	17,800	20,700
	5	0	1,700	2,800	5,000	7,600	10,700	13,700	16,600	19,500
	6	0	200	2,100	4,000	6,300	9,400	12,300	15,300	18,200
$60,000										
FAMILY SIZE	3	$1,300	3,200	4,100	7,900	10,600	14,100	16,700	19,600	22,700
	4	700	2,500	3,200	6,700	9,400	12,900	15,400	18,300	21,400
	5	300	1,900	2,500	5,500	8,200	11,700	14,200	17,200	20,200
	6	0	1,200	1,700	4,500	6,800	10,400	12,900	15,800	18,800
$80,000										
FAMILY SIZE	3	$1,800	3,800	5,800	9,000	11,800	14,900	17,800	20,700	23,700
	4	900	3,000	4,700	7,700	10,500	13,600	16,500	19,400	22,400
	5	400	2,400	3,900	6,400	9,300	12,400	15,400	18,200	21,200
	6	0	1,700	3,100	5,200	7,900	11,100	14,000	16,800	19,900

FIGURE 10.1 (CONTINUED)

ASSETS		INCOME BEFORE TAXES								
		$20,000	30,000	40,000	50,000	60,000	70,000	80,000	90,000	100,000
$100,000										
FAMILY SIZE	3	$2,800	4,000	6,900	10,200	12,900	16,000	19,000	21,800	24,800
	4	1,500	3,200	5,700	8,900	11,600	14,800	17,700	20,500	23,500
	5	900	2,500	4,700	7,500	10,400	13,600	16,500	19,300	22,300
	6	400	1,800	3,800	6,100	9,100	12,200	15,100	18,000	21,000
$120,000										
FAMILY SIZE	3	$3,900	4,900	8,000	11,300	14,000	17,100	21,000	23,200	25,800
	4	2,600	4,000	6,500	10,100	12,700	15,900	18,800	21,700	24,600
	5	1,900	3,200	5,400	8,800	11,500	14,700	17,600	20,500	23,400
	6	1,200	2,500	4,300	7,200	10,200	13,300	16,300	19,200	22,400
$140,000										
FAMILY SIZE	3	$4,600	5,900	9,200	12,400	15,400	18,200	21,200	23,800	28,200
	4	3,200	4,800	7,800	11,100	13,900	17,000	19,900	21,900	26,900
	5	2,500	3,900	6,400	9,800	12,700	15,800	18,800	21,700	25,700
	6	1,700	3,200	5,200	8,300	11,300	14,500	17,400	20,300	23,300

Source: Peterson's College Money Handbook 1998. Copyright © 1997 by Peterson's. 800-338-3282 or www.petersons.com. Reprinted with permission.

students can apply for available scholarship funds by filing an FAF, but some have a separate form specifically for scholarships.

ASK UNCLE SAM

The federal government is the single largest source of financial aid for students, spending over $20 billion per year. (See Figure 10.2.) Most of that money is reserved for families "in need," which means you may not qualify for much of this cash, if you qualify at all. Here's the lowdown on the major federal financial aid programs:

Grants are gifts from the government; you don't have to repay them. But this free money is based purely on financial need, not academic achievement. The size of the grant decreases as your family income increases. The *Pell Grant*, which is the largest federal grant program, awards about four million students annually with up to $2,340 per year. If you're applying for government aid, this is the place to start. (It's a prerequisite, in fact, for getting a government-subsidized student loan.) All you have to do is check a box on the standard financial aid form.

The *Federal Supplemental Educational Opportunity Grant* (FSEOG) awards additional need-based money to supplement the Pell Grant. The difference between Pells and FSEOGs? The government guarantees that a school will get enough money for all its Pell Grant awards, whereas it gets only a fixed amount for FSEOGs. Basically, these grants are doled out on a first-come, first-served basis. The

FIGURE 10.2   AT A GLANCE: FEDERAL FINANCIAL AID PROGRAMS

PROGRAM	MAXIMUM AWARD PER YEAR
Pell Grant	$2,340
Federal Supplemental Educational Opportunity Grant (FSEOG)	$4,000
Perkins Loan	$3,000
Stafford Loan (subsidized)	$2,625 (first year)
Stafford Loan (nonsubsidized)	$2,625 (first year)
Parent Loans for Undergraduate Students (PLUS)	Up to the cost of the education
Work-study	No maximum

maximum award is $4,000 per year, but the amount that your student ultimately receives depends on how much grant money the college has available. Both Pells and FSEOGs are for undergraduates only.

Like grants, government-subsidized *loans* are awarded to students in need. But, unlike grants, this money must be paid back. Interest rates are low, and there are no interest payments while in school. Repayment generally begins one to nine months after the student leaves college. Often, you can take up to 10 years to repay the loan. If you don't qualify for a subsidized loan, you may apply for an *unsubsidized* loan: a similarly good deal except that interest starts accruing as soon as you receive the loan, so you must begin making interest payments immediately.

A Perkins Loan is cheap, cheap, cheap. Students can borrow up to $3,000 per year at a 5% interest rate. Uncle Sam pays the interest while your student is in college, and Junior may take up to 10 years to repay the loan after graduation. Payment can be deferred even longer if the graduate joins the Peace Corps or teaches at an inner-city school. The trouble is, you can't apply for a Perkins Loan on your own. It's awarded by the college to lower-income students as part of a financial aid package.

Stafford Loans are the "student loans" of old. Your student can borrow up to $2,625 the first year of college; $3,500 for the second year; and up to $5,500 for each of the remaining two or three years that it takes to graduate. (Graduate students can borrow up to $8,500 per year of graduate study, up to a maximum of $65,000.) The interest rate: 8% for the first four years, 10% thereafter. These loans come in subsidized and nonsubsidized versions. Again, the main difference is that with a subsidized loan the government pays the interest during the college years, while with an unsubsidized loan interest payments begin immediately.

To apply for a Stafford Loan, you must fill out a separate loan application and submit it to a commercial lender such as a bank, credit union, or savings and loan association. While it's up to you to find a government-approved lender, the school should be able to give you a list of suitable lenders in your area.

Parent Loans for Undergraduate Students (PLUS) is, as its name implies, a loan for parents. You borrow the money on your child's behalf and—as you might expect—you're responsible for paying Uncle Sam back. Monthly repayments generally start 60 days after you borrow the money. You apply directly to banks, savings and loans, and credit unions (just as you do with a Stafford Loan). There is no "needs" test, but the lender will likely do a credit check. A PLUS has a variable interest rate that can't exceed 9%. More good news: There is no limit as to how much you can borrow. In some cases, you can finance the entire cost of your child's education, less any other financial aid received.

Work-study programs, such as *Federal Work-Study* (FWS), are different from both loans and grants. With this type of financial aid, students work at an on- or off-campus job to earn money to pay for school. The government subsidizes a portion of the paycheck; the college or employer pays the rest. The student works on an hourly basis and earns at least the minimum wage.

AND THE SCHOLARSHIP GOES TO . . .

Not all financial aid is based on need. Some colleges, corporations, community organizations, and churches offer money based on merit. For gifted students who are smart (but not necessarily geniuses), athletic, or artistic, scholarships can provide several hundred to thousands of dollars in tuition money each year.

The most widely publicized merit-based scholarships are the National Merit Scholarships. Some two thousand top winners are named each year, but another 4,500 runners-up also receive some money awarded by individual colleges and major corporations (mainly for children of their own employees). To qualify, kids must take the Preliminary Scholastic Aptitude Test (PSAT) in their junior year of high school.

Many corporations, as well as labor unions, offer additional scholarships to children of their employees or to students in the local community. Other community and civic groups, such as the American Legion, the 4-H Club, Rotary International, even the Girl Scouts, offer up to several thousand dollars to promising students. Some restrictions may apply: Sometimes money is given to members' children only or the funds must be used to pursue a certain field of study.

Frequently, colleges use academic scholarships as a recruiting device by offering a child who has a certain grade point average or class rank a scholarship, especially if the school is trying to attract brighter students to its campus. Other schools offer awards to students after the applicant has been accepted. That could spell good news for you. If the college really wants your daughter, it may even raise the award—if you know how to bargain.

Colleges also offer full or partial scholarships to students with special skills like acting or music. Of course, there are always athletic scholarships, too. Your kid doesn't have to be a football star to qualify, either; schools do offer athletic scholarships for less high-profile sports like swimming, volleyball, and lacrosse.

For students who're willing to do time in the armed

forces, U.S. military academies offer free education to students who pass their rigorous admissions process and commit to serve after graduation. If your child wants a nonmilitary school, your local Army, Navy, Air Force, or Marines recruiting center should have information about the Reserve Officer Training Corps (ROTC) programs at colleges. ROTC can provide lots of monetary assistance, if not a free education; but, again, your child must commit to a number of years of active duty afterward.

Before your child accepts any award, check to see if the scholarship is renewable. Some colleges offer students a generous award for the first year, but reduce it for the subsequent years. In addition, a scholarship may not mean as much money as you think it does. Some schools reduce any grants they would have given a student by the amount of outside scholarship money the student receives. So you end up paying the same amount—with or without the scholarship. A few schools, however, let you use the scholarship money to reduce your "expected family contribution." Obviously, if you don't qualify for any aid or if you have to take out a loan, a scholarship may be the best deal in town.

To find out what scholarships are available at 1,200 schools across the United States, check out *The A's and B's of Academic Scholarships* (Octameron Associates, P.O. Box 2748, Alexandria, VA 22301; 703-836-5480; $7.50 plus $2 postage fee). You might also try a computerized service. Some are very costly (up to $200), and you may end up with a list of awards that your child has only a remote chance of winning. You probably won't learn anything from these services that you couldn't find out on your own, though, either by doing some research in the library or talking with the school's guidance counselor.

THE BEST PLACES TO BORROW

You've saved as much as you could. Your child has applied for every type of government aid, scholarship, grant, and work-study program that exists. Still, you're coming up short. How do you come up with the extra money? Borrow it. But keep in mind that all loans must be paid back, with interest. And you may be putting yourself in debt at a time when you don't have many years left to work. This is the most expensive way to send a kid to college, but for some folks, it may be their only option. Here are some possibilities:

BORROWING AGAINST HOME EQUITY

If you own a home, you may be able to borrow against the equity in your house to pay for college. This kind of borrowing is especially attractive because the interest rate is generally low, and the interest paid on this loan—unlike other consumer loans—is tax-deductible, up to $100,000.

In most cases, you can borrow up to 80% of your home's equity. (That's your home's current value minus what you owe on your mortgage.) If your house is worth $200,000, for example, and you owe $75,000 on your mortgage, you have $125,000 in equity in your house. That means you can probably borrow up to 80% of $125,000, or $100,000.

Home equity borrowing comes in two basic types: the home equity loan and the home equity line of credit. The home equity loan works much like your first mortgage. (In fact, it's often referred to as a second mortgage.) You borrow a fixed amount of money, which you receive in a lump sum. You repay the loan in monthly installments over a fixed period, generally 10 or 15 years. The interest rate can be fixed or variable. You have to pay points and closing costs, just like you did when you got that first mortgage.

A home equity line of credit, on the other hand, works like a revolving credit line typical of most major credit cards. At the outset, you're approved for a certain amount of money. For the next five or ten years, you can draw on that credit line, in full or in part, whenever you want. Your monthly payments are normally a percentage (about 2%) of the outstanding balance of the line. Typically, you then have 10 or 20 years to pay back the borrowed funds.

The drawbacks of these types of loans? You're basically hocking the house. If you don't make the payments, the bank will grab your home.

REFINANCING YOUR HOME MORTGAGE

Instead of taking out a home equity loan, you can tap into your home's equity in another way: Refinance your mortgage. A "cash-out refi" lets you trade in your current mortgage for a larger one and pocket the extra money to pay for Suzie's college tuition. However, this is a time-consuming process (often, it takes as long as obtaining a first mortgage does). And, in most cases, you must pay closing costs of $500 to $5,000. Generally, this isn't a good source of funding unless you were planning on refinancing anyway to take advantage of lower mortgage interest rates.

LOANS FROM RETIREMENT PLANS

If you have a 401(k) (or its sister plan, a 403(b), which is offered to teachers and hospital workers), you can borrow up to 50% of your account's assets, up to $50,000. You generally must pay this loan back within five years. Otherwise, the loan is considered a withdrawal, and you'll owe regular income taxes plus a 10% penalty on the borrowed amount. Another drawback is that if you leave your job, you may have to pay the money back, in full, within 60 days.

There are some benefits, though. First, the money kept in a retirement account doesn't show up on a financial aid form. Stashing money in your 401(k) might actually be one way to save for college and also increase your child's chances of getting a grant or some other type of financial aid. Second, since you're essentially borrowing your own money, you pay the interest back to yourself. A loan, therefore, won't stop your retirement nest egg from growing if you pay the money back.

LOANS AGAINST A LIFE INSURANCE POLICY

You can borrow up to 90% of your policy's cash value. (Term insurance doesn't have a cash value, though, so you can't borrow against it.) You don't need to pay the loan back—ever. The loan (plus interest) will simply be subtracted from the face value of the policy that's paid to your beneficiaries when you die. Trouble is, life insurance is bought as protection for your family. Should you die before the loan is paid back, your family's financial security could be at risk.

BORROWING AGAINST STOCKS AND BONDS

You take out a "margin loan" against your stocks and bonds. How much you can borrow depends on the limits set by your brokerage firm. For instance, you can generally borrow up to 50% of the value of certain stocks, up to 85% of municipal bonds, and up to 95% of U.S. Treasuries. Getting a margin loan is quick, too. Unlike home equity loans, there are no closing costs, no preset repayment schedules, and no lengthy applications to complete. But there is always the possibility of a margin call. If the market suddenly drops (and your stocks take a beating), you'll have to repay all or part of the loan within a few days—or lose your stock.

PERSONAL LOANS

You can always consider just borrowing money from a bank. But the interest paid on an unsecured loan, which is based on your salary, is generally much higher than the interest paid on a loan that's secured with some collateral, such as your home or stocks and bonds. The most expensive kind of personal loan is a cash advance on your credit card. It's *not* an option for financing college costs, except maybe to buy books if you're temporarily strapped for cash.

QUESTIONS AND ANSWERS

Q. Is it really wise to save so much for college? Won't a sizable savings hurt my chances of getting financial aid?

A. The size of your student-aid package is based somewhat on assets, but your current income plays a bigger factor. If your income is relatively high, your expected contribution will be, too—regardless of your assets. What's more, financial aid packages usually involve loans because they don't cover the entire price of education. If you have no savings to draw on, you'll simply have to borrow more or pay the shortfall out of your current income. And that can be quite expensive, especially if you're nearing retirement or have more than one child in college at a time.

Q. How does financial aid work in cases of divorce?

A. The financial aid application should be completed by the custodial parent. Public institutions will look at just the custodial parent's finances when calculating how much aid they'll give. But private schools—which aren't bound by federal financial regulations—usually ask for information about the noncustodial parent, too. In fact, they routinely factor in both parents' incomes, even if there's little chance that the noncustodial parent will chip in. In addition, if one or both parents has remarried, some private colleges may take the stepparents' finances into account, too. All of this probably means that getting financial aid is just that much more difficult if you and your spouse split up.

Q. When my daughter first went to college, we applied for financial aid but were denied because our expected family contribution was too high to qualify. Now, my son is a high school senior and we'll soon have two in college. Will we be denied again?

A. It depends. Both your son and daughter should apply for aid next year. Your calculated expected family contribution amount is divided in half for each child when you have two in college, so may qualify because of that new lower figure.

Q. Is it possible to change your financial aid package?

A. Yes. Most colleges have some sort of appeals system. While requests for more grant money are rarely approved, you might be able to change a loan to a work-study, if the funds are available.

FOR MORE INFO

Contact the *USA Group Guarantee Services* at 800-824-7044 for information on student loans and government-approved lenders in your area.

For the latest information on applying for federal aid, check out *The Student Guide,* which is issued each year by the U.S. Department of Education. For a free copy, contact: Federal Student Aid Information Center, P.O. Box 84, Washington, DC 20044-0084; 800-433-3243; www.ed.gov.

The *AmeriCorps* program provides full-time educational awards in return for work in community service. Contact

AmeriCorps at: The Corporation for National and Community Service, 1201 New York Avenue NW, Washington, DC 20525; 800-942-2677; www.americorps.org.

Some reference books you might want to buy or check out in the library or the high school guidance counselor's office include:

The College Cost Book; *The College Handbook*; *The College Index Book*: College Board Publications, Two College Way, P.O. Box 1100, Forrestor City, VA 25438; 800-323-7155; $42, plus postage, for the three-volume set.

Don't Miss Out and *Earn and Learn* ($8 and $5, respectively; add $2 for postage); Octameron Associates, P.O. Box 2748, Alexandria, VA 22301; 703-836-5480; www.octameron.com.

The College Money Handbook; $26.95; Peterson's, P.O. Box 2123, Princeton, NJ 08543-2123; 800-338-3282; www.petersons.com.

CHAPTER ELEVEN

Your Little Tax Deduction

You've just given birth to a bouncing baby boy or girl. Uncle Sam is so delighted that he's decided to give you—and all the other new parents this year—a most generous gift: a tax deduction that you can use every year for the next 18 years (or longer, if your child goes to college or graduate school). Small wonder, then, why many parents refer to their child as "my little tax deduction."

The tax side of parenting involves more than just that $2,650 exemption, however. As a parent, not only can you claim each of your brood as a dependent but you can also claim their medical expenses as a deduction and you may even qualify for a child care tax credit if you spend money to have someone watch your child while you work. Will knowing the laws actually save you money in taxes? Probably. At the very least, you'll be able to make sounder financial decisions that will affect you and your kids in the short and the long term.

WHO'S AN EXEMPTION?

As a parent, you can get a tax exemption for every child in your family. You also get an exemption for yourself, your spouse, and any other person, such as an aging parent, that you support and who otherwise qualifies as a dependent. The personal exemption amount, which is adjusted for inflation each year, was $2,650 in 1997. Because it's a *deduction*, an exemption is deducted from your income before computing your tax. That means your taxable income is reduced by $2,650 for each dependent child in your family—plus yourself and your spouse.

That could save you some tax dollars, depending on your taxable income and your tax rate. Generally, the higher your income level (up to a certain point) and the higher your marginal tax rate, the more you benefit from these, and other, deductions.

But how do you know if your child qualifies as an exemption? He or she must pass the following five-part test:

1. *Is the child a relative or member of your household?*

   Obviously, your children pass this test automatically. So do stepchildren, adopted children, and foster children if they live with you for one year and you pay more than half of their support. But who gets to claim the child in case of divorce? The general rule is that the parent who had custody for the greater part of the year gets to claim the exemption. Do you and your spouse share joint custody? The IRS doesn't care. Only one of you can claim the child as a deduction.

   A noncustodial parent may claim their child as a deduction, however, if the other parent agrees to it. The custodial parent has to sign Form 8332, Release of Claim to Exemption for Child of Divorced or Separated Parents, which basically says that you will not claim the child's exemption for that year. You don't need to sign this form, however, if your divorce decree was made before 1985 and stipulates that the noncustodial parent gets the exemption.

2. *Is the child a citizen or resident?*

Your dependent must be a citizen or resident of the United States, Canada, or Mexico. If you're a U.S. citizen but the foreign-born child you've legally adopted is not, you can take the exemption if the child lived in your home for the entire year.

3. *Did your child file a joint return with someone else?*

If your grown son is married and filed a joint return, you can't claim him as a dependent—even if you provided financial support for him, his pregnant wife, their twin boys, and their cat. The only exception: Your son filed a joint return with his wife solely to claim a tax refund.

4. *Did the child earn more than $2,550 during the year?*

This test doesn't apply if your child is under age 19 or a full-time student under age 24. But it does apply to your college grad who has returned to the nest while he's figuring out what to do with his life—and eating you out of house and home in the meantime—if he earned more than $2,550 during the year.

5. *Did you provide more than half of your child's support this year?*

The usual things like food, shelter, clothing, and tuition count as support. The IRS allows you to include other "less obvious" expenditures, too: charitable contributions made on behalf of your child, entertainment costs such as movie tickets and spending money, and even the money you borrowed to pay for your daughter's wedding.

If your child passes all five parts of this test, you still might not be entitled to this exemption. Personal exemptions are phased out for high-income families. If you're married and filing jointly, personal deductions are reduced by 2% for every $2,500 of your adjusted gross income above $181,800. (A single taxpayer's exemption starts getting reduced when income hits $121,200; for a head of household, the figure is $151,500; for a married couple filing separate returns, it's $90,900.)

CLAIMING YOUR MEDICAL EXPENSES AS A DEDUCTION

Almost any medical or dental expense qualifies as a deduction these days. You can write off the costs of doctors' fees, hospital expenses, therapy, nursing services, medical insurance premiums, and prescription drugs. Even less obvious expenses such as abortion, birth control pills, guide dogs, cab fare to and from the doctor's office, false teeth, and contact lenses qualify. The IRS draws the line, however, at medical expenses that boost your overall general health, such as a gym membership or a weight-loss program, or those that simply make you look better, such as a hair transplant or a face-lift.

The trouble is, while most of your expenses may qualify, it's difficult to actually take the deduction on your tax return. Here's why: First, calculate your total allowable expenses. Next, subtract any reimbursements you received from your insurance company. The result is your total medical expenses. Now comes the real kick in the pants: You can deduct only that part of those expenses that exceeds 7.5% of your adjusted gross income. In other words, someone with an adjusted gross income of $20,000 would have to have more than $1,500 (or 7.5%) of nonreimbursed medical expenses before being able to deduct any of them.

But what does this have to do with your kids? Obviously, you can deduct medical and dental expenses for your kids, as well as yourself and your spouse. But more importantly, even if you can't claim your child as a dependent (because he or she earned more than $2,550 this year), you may still deduct medical expenses you paid. The same rule applies if both you and your ex share joint custody. Each parent can deduct the amount that he or she paid for the child's medical care.

CHILD CARE TAX CREDITS

If you pay someone (on the books) to care for your kids while you work, you probably can claim a child care credit on your federal income taxes. Unlike a tax deduction that merely reduces the amount of income you're taxed on, a tax credit is subtracted dollar-for-dollar from the amount of federal income tax that you owe.

To qualify, you (and your spouse, if you're married) must both work full- or part-time. Most child care expenses that benefit your child, such as the wages you pay a nanny, are allowed, but they must be incurred while you're at work or looking for work. (You can also count your share of the federal and state employment taxes you pay on a nanny's behalf as an expense.) There are some exceptions, of course. Transportation costs to and from the day care center don't qualify. An au pair's salary does qualify, but just the part spent on child care; the portion that compensates for cooking, vacuuming, and other chores doesn't. And sending your kid to a sleep-away camp is *not* a work-related expense, according to the IRS.

How much credit can you deduct? The most you're allowed is a percentage of $2,400 of expenses for one child; $4,800 for two kids or more. That doesn't mean you get the whole $2,400 or $4,800, though—just between 20% and 30% of that amount. The exact percentage that you're entitled to depends on your adjusted gross income (AGI). (You'll find that number on line 32 of Form 1040 or line 17 of Form 1040A.) Basically, the lower your AGI is, the higher the percentage you can claim. If your AGI is $10,000 or less, you'll get the whole 30 percent. If your AGI exceeds $28,000, you can claim just 20 percent.

Many states also allow a separate credit. New York, for example, allows a credit equal to 20% of the federal credit. To be eligible for it, your child must be under age 13. (Dependents, regardless of age, who are physically or mentally handicapped are also eligible.)

You can claim the federal credit on Form 2441, Child and Dependent Care Expenses. You must report the name, address, and taxpayer identification number (Social Security number, generally) of your child care provider on this form. So if you pay your nanny off the books, you *cannot* claim this tax credit.

As of 1997, there's a new credit for adoptions. Taxpayers can claim a credit against their taxes for the first $5,000 of qualifying expenses such as attorney's fees paid to adopt an eligible child. The credit is raised to $6,000 for the adoption of a special needs child. After 2001, however, the credit will apply to special needs kids *only*. It will not apply to the adoption of a foreign-born child.

Like the child care credit, the adoption credit is income-related. You'll qualify for the full credit, if you and your spouse have adjusted gross income of $75,000 or less. Higher incomes are subject to a gradual phaseout of the credit. When you reach $115,000 in income, the credit is eliminated entirely. To get the credit, file Form 8839.

FILING STATUS

Most people know whether they're married, divorced, or single. But many taxpayers—especially divorced couples—don't know if they can claim the "head of household" status, too, which offers a lower tax rate and a higher deduction than if you file as a single person. You're a likely candidate if you have a child and you pay more than half the cost of maintaining a home in which you and that child live for more than six months every year. Even if your ex claims the child as a dependent and pays you alimony and child support, you may still be able to claim a head of household status. You must be single, however, or at least living apart from your spouse for the past six months to qualify.

TAX RETURNS FOR KIDS

The tax laws used to be simpler—at least for kids. Since 1987, however, children now must frequently file tax returns on interest earned from an investment in their names (called unearned income). Often, they must also file a return for money they've earned at a job (called earned income). The requirements are confusing. Before you push your two-year-old to model the latest diapers or plunk a whole lot of money into a mutual fund account with your child's name on it, you need to know how the government taxes kids.

UNEARNED INCOME

Many kids must now file tax returns on money earning interest in their names. According to the IRS, unearned income includes any money not received as wages or compensation for a job, such as interest earned on investments; gifts of cash, stocks, or bonds; prize money; scholarship money; and Social Security survivor's benefits.

How much your child must pay to Uncle Sam depends on age and the amount earned through those investments. The first $650 in unearned income every year is completely tax-free. (The child doesn't even have to file a return.) The second $650 is taxed at 15 percent, the lowest bracket for federal income tax. After that, it's a bit more convoluted. If a child is under age 14, any unearned income above that first $1,300 is taxed at the rate the child's parents pay on their own income. Known as the Kiddie Tax, it's meant to discourage parents from sheltering investments in their child's name. When kids turn 14, however, they pay the child's tax rate (usually 15 percent) on any unearned income above $1,300.

Often, you don't have to file a separate return for a child who's under age 14. You can simply report his or her unearned income (that's interest plus dividends) on your return. To do so, you must file Form 8814, Parent's Election to Report Child's Interest and Dividends, along with your own 1040 Form. (A child whose unearned income exceeds $6,500, however, must file his or her own return.)

EARNED INCOME

If your teenager has a summer job or your toddler works as a model, he or she may have to pay taxes on those earnings. According to the IRS, earned income includes all wages, tips, and taxable scholarship and fellowship grants. Your child must file a tax return if earned income exceeds $5,100 (in 1997). Your child must also file a return if gross income—that's earned income plus unearned income—exceeds $650. Your child cannot claim a personal exemption, however, if you're claiming that child as a dependent on your tax return.

Fortunately, the Kiddie Tax doesn't apply to wages for a

job or other earned income. Wage-earning children are taxed at their own rate of 15% (generally), not their parents' rate. Some kids will not have to pay any tax at all, though. If your son has a summer job—and he has no other income, owed no tax last year, and expects to earn less than the standard deduction this year—he doesn't have to have income tax withheld from his weekly paychecks. Simply check boxes 6a and 6b on the W-4 withholding form that he must file when he begins work.

QUESTIONS AND ANSWERS

Q. Should I open a savings account for my child in his name, or mine?

A. That depends on why you're opening a savings account and how much you plan to put in it. Since the Kiddie Tax was put into place in 1987 (See previous section, "Tax Returns for Kids"), there's been little reason to sink large amounts of money into accounts in your child's name. You'll wind up being taxed at the same rate, no matter what you do. But if you want to teach your child how a bank account works and about the value of saving, open the account in his name. It'll get him more involved, and save you some money in taxes. Interest is still taxed at a child's rate on relatively small accounts bearing the child's name. (The first $650 earned in interest every year is tax-free.) Interest earned in an account of any size with your name on it, however, will be taxed at your rate, which probably higher.

Q. Our eight-year-old daughter is a model who earns about $10,000 each year. My ex-husband and I invest most of the money for her, in accounts we set up in her name. Does the Kiddie Tax *still apply in her case, even though she earned her investment money herself? If so, whose tax rate would apply—my ex-husband's or mine?*

A. The Kiddie Tax does still apply, unfortunately. While your daughter's wages will be taxed at a child's rate, any interest or dividends that are generated by her invested wages (which exceed $1,300 in 1997) will be taxed at your rate. Meanwhile, your daughter should probably pay tax at the rate of the parent who has custody. If you and your husband have joint custody, the rate is probably that of the parent with the higher rate.

Q. My ex-wife and I have joint custody of our two daughters. Can we both claim the deduction?

A. If only it were so. From a tax standpoint, the IRS doesn't recognize joint custody. Only one spouse may claim the deduction, even if you both provide equally for the support of the children and they spend exactly six months with you and six months with their mother. Usually, the parent who has custody for the greater part of the year is assumed to provide more than half of the child's support and is, therefore, granted the deduction. This is something you'll have to work out with your ex-wife.

Q. The IRS seems pretty lenient when it comes to allowing certain medical expenses to be deducted. I'm pregnant—can I deduct the cost of maternity clothes and childbirth classes?

A. Yes to the childbirth classes. No to the maternity clothes. Similarly, you can deduct nursing services to help you recover from a cesarean section, but nursing care for your healthy newborn doesn't qualify. The rules are a bit confusing, so check with the IRS or your accountant before declaring any medical deductions for you and your child.

Q. Can I claim a deduction for my adopted son, even though he's not officially adopted yet?

A. Yes, if he was placed in your care by an authorized adoption agency and currently lives with you. If you adopted the child privately and the adoption is not official yet, you can claim a deduction only if your son lived with you for the entire tax year.

Q. My daughter was born just after midnight the morning of January 1. For what year can I claim her as a deduction?

A. Sorry, but from a tax perspective you didn't plan your family very well. You can only claim her as a deduction starting with the current year. If she had been born just *before* midnight—of the old year—you could have claimed her as a deduction that whole year, even though she was born at the very last minute.

Q. My baby died several days after she was born. Can I claim a deduction?

A. Yes. If your child was born alive, you can claim an exemption for her that year. This is true even if the child lived only for a moment. You must have proof of a live birth, such as a birth certificate. Had your child been stillborn, however, you would not be allowed to claim the deduction.

FOR MORE INFO

The Internal Revenue Service offers a series of publications on tax matters, including: "Exemptions, Standard Deduction, and Filing Information" (publication 501); "Medical and Dental Expenses" (publication 502); "Child and Dependent Care Expenses" (publication 503); "Divorced or Separated Individuals" (publication 504). Contact the IRS during regular business hours at 800-829-3676 (800-TAX-FORM) for free copies or visit its Web site at www.irs.ustreas.gov. You can also call the tax hot line at 800-829-1040 with specific tax questions.

The Ernst & Young Tax Guide 1998 ($15.95; John Wiley & Sons, Inc., New York, NY; 800-225-5945) is the official IRS tax guide. It offers easy-to-use explanations and tax-saving tips on everything from your filing status to how to figure your tax to calculating the child care credit.

CHAPTER TWELVE

Insuring Your Family's Well-Being

You scrimp. You save. You work hard to provide a better life for your kids. Then one day you get hit by a bus (or your spouse does), and your financial plan goes down the drain. If only you'd had insurance. . . .

No one likes to think about insurance, much less spend time talking with an insurance agent and reading the fine print of the myriad policies available today. But, insurance is a necessary ingredient of your family's financial security. Without it, all those dreams of a Sweet 16 birthday bash, vacations at the shore, and a college education could be wiped out—with a single accident or illness.

As the parent of a young child, you absolutely, positively need life and disability insurance. Life insurance will help protect your spouse and kids should you die young. Disability insurance will help protect you and your family should you no longer be able to work and earn a salary. When you buy insurance, what you're really buying is peace of mind that your family is protected. It's just one of those things that you must spend money on, even though it often seems like you're just throwing that money out the window. Once you fit those insurance premiums into your budget, though, you can forget about what will happen if tragedy strikes—and get on with the business of living.

LIFE INSURANCE

Mention life insurance, and most folks' eyes glaze over. Perhaps it's all those actuarial charts insurance salespeople use to pitch their policies. Yet, life insurance is really quite simple. You buy it so that your family will be provided for if you die.

When you buy life insurance, you pay a premium annually, semiannually, or quarterly, just like you do with auto, medical, and other types of insurance. The cost of your premium is based on your age and your health. If you die, your beneficiary (most likely your spouse and/or kids) gets a lump sum payment, known as the death benefit.

Not everyone carries life insurance, and even those families that do often don't carry enough. According to the American Council of Life Insurance, 78% of all households carry $173,700, on average, in life insurance. That's not much, considering how much it costs to raise one child.

As a parent, you need the most life insurance when your kids are young and dependent on you for their food, shelter, and education. If you, the breadwinner, should die unexpectedly, a life insurance policy will "insure" that your family's needs—mortgage payments, child care expenses, college tuition payments—can still be met. Basically, it replaces your income should you die before your time.

Your insurance needs will change over time. As children get older and your family assets increase, you may need less insurance. (Most people find they need less insurance, for instance, once their mortgage is paid off.) You'll need more insurance if you have several children. It's smart to reevaluate your insurance coverage every few years, but especially under the following circumstances:

- Birth or adoption of a child
- Marriage or divorce
- Career or job change
- Retirement
- Purchase of a home
- Death of a family member

So, who needs insurance? Parents of young children do. Kids have to be raised and educated, and—as we're discovering—it isn't cheap. As a rule, only the breadwinner needs to be insured. (If both Mom and Dad earn a salary, then both of them need to be insured.) But in some cases, it may make sense to cover a stay-at-home parent, too. Although this spouse doesn't earn an actual income, a homemaker does cook, clean, and take care of children—all of which would cost money if the other spouse had to hire someone to do it. If your spouse couldn't afford to pay for these services after your death, then you need your own policy.

Once kids are on their own, however, you should be able to reduce your coverage, unless your child is handicapped or in some other way still dependent on you. Kids, by the way, don't need to be insured. They don't provide any income that needs to be protected, and, statistically, it's unlikely that they'll die before you. If you think that an insurance policy is a form of forced savings for college, forget about it. You'll get a far better return on your money—and a bigger college fund as a result—if you take those premiums and plunk them into a growth mutual fund instead.

How much insurance do you need? That depends on several factors: how old you are, how many children you have, the ages and educational needs of those children, how much money you have saved, the maturity of your home mortgage, your spouse's current and future earnings, and how well your family can live without your income. Some people buy enough insurance so that their family can continue their current lifestyle even after the sole breadwinner dies. Other people buy just enough insurance to tide the family over until they can make some adjustments in their lives.

Unfortunately, there is no magic number. Some experts suggest that life insurance should equal six to eight times your gross annual take-home pay. But that's just a rule of thumb, and it may not apply to your family's situation. In addition, the amount of coverage that you need will change at various stages in your life. If you have a newborn (who will, therefore, be dependent on you for the next 18 years) and your mortgage has another 20 years or so to go, you'll probably need coverage that will give your family 75% of your former after-tax income to maintain their current standard of living (60% will allow them to get by, but ultimately your spouse will probably have to find a higher-paying job and/or sell the house for a smaller place). Twenty years from now, however, when your kids are living on their own and your mortgage is paid off, you may need coverage that gives your family just 40% to 50% of your former after-tax income. This, of course, will depend on the other assets you've accumulated over those 20 years and how much of your stated coverage has been eroded by inflation.

For a true picture of your family's insurance needs, you'll need to sit down with a financial planner and/or a trusted insurance agent and do some serious calculating. (Sorry, folks, there is no quick fix here.)

Once you've determined how much insurance you need, you must pick the kind of policy that best suits your needs. A great variety of policies abound, each with its own unique features. (That's what makes buying insurance so confusing.) But, basically, life insurance falls into two main categories: term and cash value. Term insurance offers you protection, like homeowner's or auto insurance. Cash value insurance gives you protection, plus an investment fund.

Term Insurance

This is the simplest kind of insurance you can get, and generally the cheapest, too. What you're buying is protection should you die—period. You pay annual or semiannual premiums for a certain period of time, generally 10, 15, or 20 years. In return, your spouse and kids collect a set amount, or *death benefit*, if you die during the term of the policy.

Should you outlive the term of the policy (and not renew it beforehand), however, you get nothing. Unlike other insurance policies, a term policy is not an investment. You can't borrow against this policy, or surrender it for some cash, because there is no cash buildup. This no-frills policy is worthless when you stop making the premium payments or at the end of its term.

Still, term policies are generally the best bet for young parents because they provide the most coverage—for the lowest cost—at the time you need it most: when your kids are young and depend on you for their support. A 30-year-old man, for instance, would pay $171 annually for a 30-year guaranteed term policy that would pay $100,000 upon death. A whole-life policy with the same death benefit would cost $500 in premiums the first year.

When you buy term insurance, you can buy it with level

(the same) premiums for one year. That's called *annual re-newable term.* Other policies specify the term: generally 10, 15, or 20 years. Your premium remains the same for the entire term. (This type of policy will cost a little more to start but may be cheaper over the long term.) Many policies are renewable term after term, until you reach age 70 or so. (But not always. Be sure to check this out.) Expect to pay steeper premiums as you get older. Why? Statistically, you're more likely to die than you were, say, 20 years ago.

In addition to the standard term policy, you'll find two other types of term available: *decreasing term insurance* and *increasing term insurance.* With a decreasing term policy, your premiums stay the same over the life of the policy but your death benefit decreases. This often appeals to young couples, because they expect their family expenses to be lower later on in life. (For most people, that's because their mortgage is paid off.) An increasing term policy, on the other hand, increases the death benefit over time (and, thus, guards against inflation). The premiums increase, of course, along with the coverage.

Whatever kind of term policy you choose, look to see if it offers a *guaranteed conversion.* This lets you convert your term policy into a cash value policy without taking another medical exam. Generally, this provision may cost you a bit extra but it'll allow you to continue your coverage into old age, even if your health deteriorates. You might also want to consider a *guaranteed renewability feature.* That means you can renew your policy automatically, regardless of your health. (Again, you won't have to take another medical exam. This is especially important as you get older and your health declines.)

CASH VALUE INSURANCE

Also known as permanent insurance, cash value policies offer traditional life insurance protection plus a tax-deferred savings feature. A good portion of your premium buys you some life insurance; the remainder is deposited into an account that earns interest like any other investment.

The money earned on the account is yours, even if you cancel the policy. Should your insurance needs change and you no longer want the coverage, for instance, you can cash in your policy. This surrender value, however, is less than the face value, which is the amount of money (written on the face of the policy) that's paid at death.

In addition, you can borrow money from your policy, using the cash value in the policy as collateral for the loan. Should you die before you pay back the loan, your death benefit will be reduced by the amount owed.

Insurance companies offer several different kinds of cash value policies. There are three basic types: whole-life insurance, universal life insurance, and variable life insurance.

WHOLE-LIFE INSURANCE

Also called ordinary life or straight life insurance, whole-life is the most common type of cash value insurance. Your premiums, which are based on the age at which you buy the policy, stay the same for your entire lifetime. (Therefore, the younger you are when you buy a whole life policy, the cheaper the premiums.) Your death benefit is a fixed amount, too. The insurance stays in force until you die. And a portion of your premiums earn interest and grow tax-deferred, building a cash value over time. In the future, you can borrow against this money, or simply cash in the policy and withdraw the accumulated savings.

If you buy whole-life insurance when you're young, it'll cost you more than a comparable amount of term insurance during the first few years. As you get older, however, your rates won't increase, and you'll wind up paying less in premiums than someone who's renewing a term policy. Should you no longer want to make those premium payments, the insurance company can then deduct them from the policy's cash value.

UNIVERSAL LIFE INSURANCE

A universal life policy is generally cheaper than a whole-life policy, but costlier than a term policy. It also generally offers a more competitive interest rate (on your cash value) than a comparable whole-life policy. Its main draw, though, is its flexibility. After your initial payment, you can pay premiums at any time, in any amount, to suit your needs. (Typically, you're subject to specified minimums and maximums.) The insurance company will often recommend a target premium, but you're free to make a larger payment this month, then skip the next two months. If you don't pay enough in any one month to cover the cost of your coverage, the money will be subtracted from your cash value.

You can also choose the size of your death benefit. Option 1 gives you lower death benefits and a larger cash buildup. Option 2 gives you a smaller cash buildup and higher death benefits. You can start with one option (the higher death benefit is of greater necessity, for instance, when the kids are young) and then switch to the other option later on.

VARIABLE LIFE INSURANCE

This type of insurance lets you decide how your cash value dollars are invested. Most policies offer a variety of stock, bond, or mutual fund investment choices, which you, the policyholder, pick yourself. (The choices are generally mutual funds managed by the insurance company.) You can shift your money from one investment option to another during certain periods each year.

Your death benefit rises and falls with your investment's

performance, too, but it will never fall below the original amount of insurance coverage spelled out in your policy. In most cases, variable life insurance costs more than both whole-life and universal life insurance.

TERM VS. CASH VALUE INSURANCE

Which is better? For most parents, plain old term insurance works best. You get far more coverage for your money than you do from cash value insurance, so it's generally the ideal insurance for parents with average incomes and dependent kids. The cost of term insurance rises as you age, however. Most folks aged 60 or older can't afford to carry this type of policy. But, presumably, by that time you won't need insurance. Your kids will be living on their own; and you'll have a pension, savings, and/or Social Security to pay your funeral bills and support your spouse.

Cash value policies, on the other hand, generally cover longer-term needs because term insurance becomes too expensive as you get older. This kind of policy may work better for you if you need to keep your coverage into old age, or you have a higher-than-average income. The premiums for cash value insurance are more costly than those of term insurance in the early years, but they remain the same for life. You'll pay the same premium when you're 75 as you did when you were 25. Often, these are the only policies that people can afford to carry into their 70s and 80s. Why would you need insurance then? Your savings and/or pension isn't enough to take care of your spouse or a handicapped child.

If money is not an issue and you can afford all of the coverage that you need, a cash value policy might be a reasonable place to invest some of your long-term money. You must look at these investments carefully, though. The stated interest rates are deceptive. Under no circumstances should

SHOP BY PHONE

If you're in the market for a new insurance policy, you can comparison-shop by phone. Simply call up one of the following computerized price-quote services. After you provide some basic information, such as your health, age, and the amount of insurance required, they'll tap into their vast database of policies from different insurance companies and find you the least expensive policies that meet your needs. The service is usually free of charge. You can buy your policy from these services, too, but you're under no obligation to do so.

Insurance Quote Services: 3200 North Dobson Road, Building C, Chandler, AZ 85224; 800-972-1104; www.iquote.com

SelectQuote Insurance Services: 595 Market Street, 6th Floor, San Francisco, CA 94105; 800-343-1985; www.selectquote.com

TermQuote: 6768 Loop Road, Centerville, OH 45459; 800-444-8376; www.term-quote.com

Quotesmith: 8205 South Cass Avenue, Suite 102, Darien, IL 60561; 800-556-9393; www.quotesmith.com

such a policy be your first—or only—place to accumulate savings on a tax-deferred basis. Look instead to a 401(k) plan or an individual retirement account.

DISABILITY INSURANCE

What would happen if you couldn't work for the next six months or year? For the rest of your life?

Your savings would probably be wiped out. Your house would go into foreclosure. Your spouse would have to work three jobs just to make ends meet. And the kids wouldn't make it to college, never mind medical school.

Unless, of course, you had disability insurance. Although you probably never think of it as an asset, your earning power is the most powerful asset that you own. And, like other assets, it should be fully insured. As the parent of a dependent child, you need disability insurance for the same reason that you need life insurance: to replace your income. Only in this situation you haven't died. You've just suffered a heart attack or a stroke, been hurt in a car accident, or fallen off the roof and broken your hip, and you can't work for an extended period of time. Not only will your family have to do without your income, they'll have to stretch the family's budget even further to cover the additional medical expenses that will arise during your recuperation.

If you're like most folks, you probably have some disability coverage already. Many companies give you paid sick leave or actual disability insurance payments if you can't work for a while. Others offer standard short-term disability coverage for 26 weeks. (Generally, your employer will foot this bill.) Some offer longer-term disability plans; but many don't. (For long-term disability, the employer and employee will often split the price of the premium.)

This is where you come in. Generally, the coverage provided by your employer or through workers' compensation isn't enough. You need to supplement it with an individual policy.

How much is enough? You can never buy too much disability insurance—literally. An insurer won't sell you a policy that covers more than your gross income. In fact, many insurers won't sell you even that much because they feel it destroys any incentive to work (you could almost make money by being disabled). Instead, they'll give you a policy that covers a percentage of your former income. Your policy is given in monthly dollar amounts. You might buy a policy, for instance, that pays $2,000 per month.

Since disability benefits that you buy yourself are tax-free,

HOW TO BUY INSURANCE

Buying insurance is almost as difficult as buying a used car. You want the best deal, for the least amount of money. The salespeople want to make a sale, and will do anything to convince you they have the product you need. But do they?

Insurance salespeople (or agents) work on a commission basis. The more they get you to buy, the more they earn. So no matter how qualified or professional an agent is, you're still likely to hear some hype, especially about more expensive products.

To make an intelligent decision, you first need to understand what kind of agent you're dealing with. *Exclusive agents* or *direct agents* work for one particular insurance company. They know that company's policies and procedures inside and out. Often, the policies that these agents offer are cheaper than those sold by independent agents because direct agents earn smaller commissions. But exclusive agents are obviously biased toward their own products. A policy offered by a competing insurer may be more suitable, but they can't tell you that. You'll have to do sufficient legwork yourself to make sure that you're getting the best policy at the best price.

Independent agents, on the other hand, represent several insurance companies. They can quote you rates and terms on a number of policies offered by a variety of insurers. (That means less work for you.) Prices may be somewhat steeper, however, because companies must pay higher commissions to get independent agents to sell their products. And you still may not be getting an unbiased opinion. Like exclusive agents, independent agents are also motivated by commission. They want to sell you as expensive a policy as they can persuade you to buy.

If you want to use an agent, ask your friends and family for a referral. Or, contact the American Society of CLU (Chartered Life Underwriters) and ChFC (Chartered Financial Consultants) at 888-CHFC-CLU. They'll randomly refer up to five chartered life insurance underwriters in your area. (Insurance agents permitted to call themselves "chartered life underwriter" must pass 10 college-level courses in insurance and must have at least three years of practical industry experience.) The National Association of Life Underwriters in Washington, DC, will likewise refer some of its member life insurance agents in your area.

In addition, you can also try your state department of insurance. Many of these agencies, which regulate insurance companies and agents within their state, publish consumer guides to insurance and cost-comparison surveys. Frequently, they'll also supply you with a list of agents in your area. Most states require that agents be licensed to sell insurance. (To check up on your agent, contact your state department of insurance.) Agents who sell variable life insurance (policies that invest some of your premiums into stocks, bonds, and/or money market funds) must also be registered with the National Association of Securities Dealers in Washington, DC (800-289-9999).

You could always cut out the intermediary and buy direct from the insurance company. Not all companies sell directly to individuals, of course. Others offer just certain types of policies. And, in some states, savings banks can sell life insurance directly to the consumer. Another possibility is the group policy, available through your employer, credit union, or professional association. These premiums are usually very low, and the coverage sound. Often, you don't need a medical exam to qualify. But coverage may be canceled abruptly if, for instance, you quit your job.

you need to buy only enough insurance to replace your take-home pay. If your employer buys a policy for you, however, those benefits are taxed. The amount of coverage you can buy depends, ultimately, on your salary. So you must adjust your coverage periodically to reflect any salary increases.

Disability insurance isn't cheap. That's why so many people don't buy it. A good policy can cost $500 to $1,500 or more per year, depending on your sex, your age, your occupation, and the amount of coverage you want. Older people pay more than younger people, for instance. People in hazardous occupations, such as firefighting and construction work, pay more than those in low-risk occupations like office work, because they're more likely to be injured on the job. And sometimes women pay more than men because the gentler sex supposedly file more disability claims.

Three other important factors affect price, too:

1. *The length of the waiting period.* The longer it takes for your policy's payments to kick in after an accident or injury, the cheaper it'll be. Waiting 90 days instead of 30 could cut your insurance premium in half.

2. *The length of the policy.* Short-term policies that pay benefits for up to two years cost a lot less than long-term policies that pay benefits for five years or more. Ideally, you want a policy to pay until age 65, when you can start collecting Social Security.

3. *How "disability" is defined.* Some policies stipulate that you can't collect benefits if you could be employed in any other job. A so-called own occupation contract will pay benefits if you're unable to work at your own job or profession, but this costs big bucks.

Shopping for disability insurance can be confusing. Details vary from one policy to another, so it may be difficult to compare them. Before buying a policy, make sure you understand what you're buying. Some crucial clauses to consider include:

Noncancelable. This guarantees your right to renew your policy every year for as long as the policy lasts. As long as you pay your premiums, the insurer can't cancel your policy. In addition, the company can't change your benefits or raise your premium. If you buy a policy that's simply "guaranteed renewable," the insurer still can't cancel your policy, but it can raise your premiums.

Guaranteed Annual Premium. Most policies offer level premiums, meaning the amount stays the same as long as the amount of coverage remains the same. But make sure. A "guaranteed annual premium" means your premium can't be increased.

Waiver of Premium. This clause means that you won't have to pay any more premiums once you're disabled.

QUESTIONS AND ANSWERS

Q. If I borrow money from my insurance policy, what happens to the investment portion of my policy?

A. Your cash value will continue to earn interest, even when you borrow against the policy. But, in many cases, it will earn interest at a lower rate than it did before. Let's assume that your whole-life policy now earns 8.5%. If you borrow money from the policy, that interest rate may be cut to 6.5% (or less) on the portion of the cash value that you've borrowed. (Most policies guarantee a minimum interest rate of 4% or 5%.)

Q. I talked to one insurance agent about a term life policy. But he didn't seem too eager to answer my questions. In fact, he kept asking if I'd considered other policies that would help me save for my three-year-old daughter's college education. Does that mean I'm not a good candidate for term? I'm 32 years old; my wife stays at home full-time.

A. Often, insurance agents don't push term policies because the low premiums don't earn them much in commission. They may try to convince you—as the agent did in your case—that you'd be better off with a cash value policy that will help you save for the future. (A cash value policy will, incidentally, earn him a heftier commission.) Since you're very young, I think you'd probably be better off buying a cheaper term policy. Take that extra money you might have put into a more expensive cash value policy and invest in stocks and mutual funds instead. Younger parents like you can afford to be more aggressive with their investments. In the end, you're likely to get a better return for your money than any insurance company would have given you. If you feel that permanent insurance is the way to go, however— and you're planning on keeping that insurance for a long time—put the cash value portion of your policy into a growth stock mutual fund. It's your only hope of taking advantage of long-term market performance.

Q. Is there any way I can check out if a cash value policy is a good investment?

A. The Consumer Federation of America can give you an unbiased analysis of cash value life insurance, for a fee. They'll evaluate any proposal you get from an insurance agent as well as help you decide if your current policy is worth keeping. Contact them at 202-387-0087. You pay $40 for the first analysis, and $30 for each additional one submitted at the same time.

Q. How do I find out if my insurance company is in good financial shape?

A. Term insurance policies always get paid, even if the insurance company goes bankrupt. But before buying any life or disability insurance policy, it's a good idea to make sure that the company is financially stable. Five major rating services track insurance companies: A. M. Best (908-439-2200); Duff & Phelps (312-368-3157); Weiss Companies (800-289-9222); Moody's Investors Service (212-553-0300); Standard & Poor's (212-208-1527). Each service grades the insurance company's financial strength, using a letter grade. Unfortunately, they don't all use the same grading system, so be sure to ask for an explanation of how they grade each company. Best uses A++, A+, A . . . , for example; Standard & Poor's uses AAA, AA+, AA. . . . You can find these ratings in the library, or you can call the rating services directly. Most of the services offer free ratings but charge for a full report.

Q. If I'm disabled won't I qualify for Social Security benefits?

A. Don't count on Social Security to pull you through. The requirements are rather stringent. To qualify, you must be completely disabled for five months and the disability has to be expected to last for at least one year. Even if you meet the requirements, however, you'll have to wait at least six months before collecting your first check.

Q. Does a disability policy cover pregnancy?

A. Generally, but there are often restrictions. Some policies cover only complications from pregnancy that require bed rest. Others will cover a normal pregnancy only *after* a 90-day waiting period. (For details, see Chapter 4.)

FOR MORE INFO

Check out these free or low-cost guides:

"Buyer's Guide to Insurance: What the Companies Won't Tell You," by the Consumer Federation of America: P.O. Box 12099, Washington, DC 20005; 202-387-6121; free, with a self-addressed envelope.

"What You Should Know About Buying Life Insurance," by the American Council of Life Insurance: 1001 Pennsylvania Avenue NW, 5th Floor, Washington, DC 20004; 202-624-2000; free.

For those with Internet access, the *Quicken InsureMarket* service (www.insuremarket.com) contains a "family needs planner" section that can help you assess your insurance needs.

Contact the *National Insurance Consumer Helpline* (800-942-4242) for free advice about life and other types of insurance. Sponsored by insurance industry trade associations, the hot line is staffed with insurance pros who'll tell you what to do if you're having trouble filing a claim, and how to buy insurance if you need it.

CHAPTER THIRTEEN

$

Will You— or Won't You?

What do you mean you don't have a will? You're the parent of two small kids and you don't have a will? Don't you know that. . . .

Okay, I admit it. I have no right to be standing up here on my soapbox. I'm the mother of three kids under the age of six, and my husband and I just drew up our own will *last week*. Dare I even mention that my brother is an attorney who specializes in estate planning?

So what's my excuse? Basically, I never thought I had enough assets to make it worth the trouble. I figured I'd get around to it sooner or later. And, frankly, I didn't plan on dying anytime soon. I still don't, of course, but when baby number three arrived—and the kids now outnumbered the grown-ups in our household—I hit upon a scary realization: Juggling three kids and a job and a home is exhausting. And I'm their *mother*. Who in their right mind would ever care for this tribe voluntarily if something should happen to me and my husband?

That's why we needed a will. And, as a parent, that's why you need one, too.

If you die intestate, or without a will, your assets will be divided by a judge in probate court according to the laws of your state. Without a will, your assets will pass automatically to your legal heirs, who may or may not be the people you'd like to see enjoying your fine wine cellar after you die. Without a will, nothing—and I mean *nothing*—will go to friends, distant relatives, charities, or even a roommate you've lived with for years. Without a will, the kids from your first marriage could go empty-handed, if you're divorced and remarried and your current spouse inherits everything.

For most married folks with kids, dying intestate might not matter all that much. Your worldly possessions will pass to the spouse and kids—which may be precisely the distribution you always had in mind anyway. But a will does more than split up your stuff. Its second function—and one that is probably of greater importance to parents of young children—is to designate a guardian for your kids. Without a will, a judge will decide who's best suited to raise the orphaned children you leave behind. That's a frightening proposition, folks. It was hard enough for *me* to make that decision—never mind a judge who doesn't know me or my kids from the next case in line.

Enough said. If you haven't written a will yet, do it now. Here's what you need to know about this important document:

WHAT A WILL DOES

A will (formally known as a "last will and testament") is simply a written document that explains who will handle your financial affairs when you die and how you want your possessions (called your estate) divided up. Your estate includes everything from your bank accounts and stock certificates to the summer home at the shore and your antique china cabinet.

Any citizen of the United States who is over age 18 and is of sound mind can write a will. You must sign your name at the bottom, in the presence of at least two witnesses who aren't beneficiaries (heirs) of the will. Witnesses must realize that you're drafting a will, but they don't need to know the contents of the will.

If you change your mind about what's in your will, you can always write a new will—as often as you like. (In the new will, however, you must state that all previous wills are revoked.) To make a minor change or two, simply add a written amendment, called a codicil. You can have an unlimited number of codicils but each must be dated, signed, and witnessed according to your state's procedures.

Since you're probably writing this will when you're young (if my sermonizing has gotten through, that is), you should review it every few years, especially if any of the following take place: (1) a new child or grandchild, by birth, adoption, or marriage; (2) marriage, separation, or divorce; (3) a change in the property or inheritance laws; (4) death of an heir or executor; and (5) a significant rise or fall in your income or financial status.

Whether you own a car, a bed, and a handful of personal items or an estate that rivals the Rockefellers' holdings, here's what you can expect a basic will to accomplish:

IT NAMES AN EXECUTOR

The executor sees that your will is carried out. The job can be simple, or quite complex, depending on the size and nature of your estate. Since he or she generally works with a lawyer, the person you name as executor needn't be a financial whiz or an expert in estate law, but should be organized and responsible about money. Some of the things the executor will have to do? Pay your debts, funeral bills, and taxes; claim your life insurance; notify your creditors; sell your property, if necessary; take inventory of your assets; deal with your heirs.

Generally, people ask someone who's named as a major beneficiary in the will to act as executor. Others choose a professional—either a bank or a lawyer. In either case, the person should be paid for the work: often 3% to 5% of the value of the estate.

Before assigning an executor, ask if the person wants the job. (You might want to assign an alternate, just in case.) Pick someone who's about your age or younger, so that there's less chance that person will die before you do. Many people name their adult children as coexecutors, especially when the estate is to be divided between them.

IT DIVVIES UP YOUR STUFF

These are your instructions basically for who gets what— and how much. When you name your heirs (referred to here as "beneficiaries"), clearly identify the recipient ("my brother, Jack") and the property ("my sapphire and diamond ring" rather than simply "my ring"). You can also leave general gifts, such as, "I leave $20,000 to the American Cancer Society."

If you're young (or even if you're not so young), you won't know now what your estate will be worth when you die. It may be best, then, to divide your estate as fractions or percentages of your estate rather than as specific sums. Let's assume that your estate is currently worth $100,000. You bequeath $20,000 to each of your four children, $5,000 to your three brothers, and $5,000 to your favorite charity. By the time you die, however, your estate may be worth twice as much, and you'd like to give a bigger chunk to your siblings and the charity. In your will, then, say: 20% goes to each child, 5% goes to each brother, and another 5% goes to the charity.

IT NAMES A GUARDIAN FOR MINOR CHILDREN

This is perhaps the toughest task of all. If you and your spouse are both killed in a car crash, who will act as surrogate parents of little Andrew and Emily? Most people choose someone who shares their values and way of life: a brother, a sister, a close friend, or a grandparent. (The trouble with a grandmother, however, is that she's older and the child is likely to be left alone again.) If you're divorced, the guardianship normally falls to your ex-spouse, as long as your ex wants it and is fit to do it (e.g., not a drug user). Obviously, before you assign a guardian, you must talk it over with that person. Is he or she willing to take on this added responsibility?

IT LIMITS YOUR ESTATE TAX LIABILITY AS MUCH AS POSSIBLE

Here's where a good estate attorney or tax specialist really comes in handy. If you're married and you die, all of your assets can be passed to your surviving spouse tax-free. That's called the *unlimited marital deduction.* But once your spouse dies—or if both you and your spouse die at the same time— your kids will be zapped with taxes, unless your attorney or a tax specialist creates a tax-saving plan for you.

SOMEDAY, SON, THIS WILL ALL BE YOURS

You want your kids to have that nest egg you've been steadily building, but you certainly don't want them to

IF YOU DON'T HAVE A WILL . . .

- The court will choose your child's guardian.
- Your favorite charity will get zip.
- Ditto for your stepchildren.
- Ditto for your friends or roommates (same sex or otherwise).
- Your entire estate might not go to your spouse, depending on state law.
- Your handicapped child may inherit money and be disqualified from government aid.
- Your family may not inherit your business, or may be forced to sell it upon your death.
- There will probably be no trust to take care of your toddler's inheritance.
- Your family may fight with each other, the courts, or both over your estate for years.

squander it all on a flashy convertible and a two-year holiday abroad. How can you leave money to your kids without giving them too much control over how it's spent?

1. *Assign a guardian of the property (or conservator) for the children's funds.*

   Perhaps your loving sister isn't financially savvy and would invest that tidy little nest egg unwisely. Maybe she just doesn't want the responsibility. No problem. Your child's guardian doesn't have to manage the support money you've left, too. You can assign someone else to look after those assets for you. It needn't be a professional money manager (but it could be). All you need is someone with good business sense.

   The *guardian of the property*, or conservator, is closely supervised by the probate court. State law determines, in fact, what can be spent on the children and what type of investments may be made. (This can be a drawback: The court may insist that all funds be kept in safe investments like a certificate of deposit when the conservator feels the assets would yield more—and not be at much risk—if invested in the stock market for 10 years.) Once the children come of age—18 or 21, depending on the state you live in—the relationship automatically ends and the kids get all the money.

2. *Use the Uniform Transfers to Minors Act (UTMA).*

If you live in one of the 38 states (or the District of Columbia) that's adopted this act, you can leave money to your child in your will and then name a custodian to manage those funds. The custodian can hold the assets until the child reaches maturity—again, age 18 or 21, depending on your state—when all funds must be turned over to the heir.

3. *Use the Uniform Gifts to Minors Act (UGMA).*

In the states that haven't adopted UTMA, you have to make a gift to your kids while you're still alive rather than in your will. You can appoint yourself as custodian, of course. The drawbacks? There are several. The gift is irrevocable: You can't get the money back once it's been given. The money may be used only to pay for your child's expenses (not yours). So, if you need the money in a few years to build up your sagging business, forget it. Finally, Junior gets the money upon maturity and is allowed to spend it as he wishes—even if that means blowing it all on a trip around the world rather than four years at Princeton.

4. *Leave the money in trust.*

With a *minor's testamentary trust*, you appoint a trustee—a relative, friend, attorney, or bank—who will manage the money for your children and make payments to them according to your wishes. Unlike the *custodial accounts* already described, however, trust funds do not automatically fall into the kids' hands at maturity. You set the date: If your kids seem immature, you can instruct the trustee to withhold their inheritance until age 25 or 30, or to make limited payments to them over the years. In addition, if you stipulate that the money placed in trust is for your daughter's college education, then that's what it will be used for. You can set up one trust for all of your children. Typically, all the money stays in trust until the youngest reaches, say, 25. Then the trust dissolves and each child gets a share.

DO YOU NEED A LAWYER?

You can draw up your own will using one of the many do-it-yourself books or computer software available today. Preprinted or computer-generated fill-in-the-blank wills (also called statutory wills) may do the job, especially if you have a simple will, such as "I want to leave everything to my wife." That'll certainly save you some money. The Quicken Family Lawyer software package will help you prepare seven different kinds of wills (and 81 other legal documents) for just $29. Lawyers, on the other hand, either bill by the hour ($150 or more) for writing a will, or charge a flat fee, which can range from $100 for a simple will to several thousand dollars for a complete estate plan.

The laws regarding inheritance are complicated, though, and filled with unforeseen traps. While there's no hard-and-fast rule as to when you need a lawyer and when you could do it yourself, you should probably consult a lawyer if you have a complicated estate, want to make unusual arrangements, or find yourself in any of the following situations:

- Your estate is worth $625,000 or more. The federal estate tax generally kicks in at this point. Although the estate can pass to your spouse tax-free, the money will be taxed when your spouse dies. A lawyer can often find ways to reduce those taxes.

- You don't know what your state's laws are. Inheritance laws vary from state to state.

- You own a business. It's not necessarily true that your share of a business will fall to your heirs.

- You want your will to be airtight. The trouble with drafting a will yourself is that one small mistake—you didn't have the right number of witnesses, for instance—could make the whole thing invalid.

- You want to disinherit someone. You can disinherit your children in every state except Louisiana. But in most states you must mention the disinherited child by name, or the court assumes you simply forgot and awards the child a portion of your estate anyway.

- You want to set up a trust.

If your lawyer charges by the hour, you can save money by doing some of the work yourself so that you'll spend less time in the office with the meter ticking. Prepare the following *before* you meet with your attorney:

- A complete list of your assets and liabilities.

- A list of your beneficiaries: family members, friends, even charities.

- What you want those beneficiaries to get. Be as specific as possible in naming personal possessions such as jewelry and collections to avoid any confusion later on.

- The names of your executor and guardians for your children.

QUESTIONS AND ANSWERS

Q. What is a living will?

A. A *living will* is a document that expresses your wishes should the need arise to be kept alive—or not—by a life-support machine or some other extraordinary means. Living wills are recognized in all 50 states and the District of Columbia, but laws about the witnesses needed and other aspects of drafting the will vary by state. For a copy of a living will for your state, contact: Choice in Dying, 200 Varick Street, New York, NY 10014; 212-366-5540. (The cost is $3.50.) Like a last will and testament, a living will can be revoked if you change your mind.

Q. What happens if my wife becomes seriously ill and can no longer make financial decisions for herself?

A. You would need a *power of attorney*. When you draw up a will, it's a good idea to draft this document, too—for both you and your spouse. A power of attorney, which must be signed, dated, and witnessed, grants your spouse, child, or whomever else you choose the ability to make financial decisions for you when you can no longer do it yourself. A power of attorney can be granted on a temporary basis (to expire after a stated period of time) or on a long-term basis. A *durable power of attorney* lasts until it is revoked.

Q. Perhaps I've been reading too many lurid news stories, but I'm worried that, after my death, my husband will remarry and his new wife will squander our savings, leaving my three kids with nothing. Is there anything I can do to prevent this from happening?

A. You could set up a Qualified Terminable Interest Property Trust, or QTIP. This would prevent the scenario you've just described. A QTIP trust gives your surviving spouse a lifetime income, but not control of your entire estate. When he dies, the trust passes on to whomever *you* choose. In this case, it would likely be your kids.

Q. Where should I store my will?

A. Give the original copy of your will to your attorney. Keep a copy in your safe-deposit box or fireproof strongbox at home. If you want, you can also give a copy to the person you've named as executor.

Q. I've named my sister as guardian of my two children. If something happens to me and the kids go live with her, would that be the same as if she had adopted them?

A. No. While both a guardian and an adoptive parent have the same basic rights and responsibilities as birth parents, a guardianship ends when the child reaches age 18. Adoption, however, is forever. It's unlikely, of course, that your sister will simply abandon your kids the day they turn 18, but, legally, she is no longer responsible for them at that point.

Q. What happens if both my sister and brother want guardianship of my 10-year-old daughter?

A. Assuming, of course, that you haven't worked this out ahead of time in your will and your sister and brother can't come to an agreement themselves, a judge must decide who'll be appointed guardian. Normally, custody is given to the surviving parent first (even in the case of divorce). Next, the court almost always places a child in the hands of another family member: an aunt, uncle, or grandparent. In this case, however, the judge would probably consider your siblings' personal situations (Are they married or single? Do they have children of their own? How are they doing financially?) as well as your daughter's relationship with each of them. Ultimately, the judge would weigh the facts, and then make a decision.

FOR MORE INFO

To find an estate planning attorney, contact:

- The National Network of Estate Planning Attorneys: 410 17th Street, Suite 1260, Denver, CO 80202; 800-638-8681.
- The Estate Planning Specialists: 3200 North Dobson Road, Building C, Chandler, AZ 85224; 800-223-9610.
- Your local Bar Association

If you need a will and are computer-literate, try one of these software packages:

The Complete Legal Collection by Quicken includes the Family Lawyer software plus the *ABA Family Legal Guide* and the *Plain Language Law Dictionary*; $49; 800-990-7222.

Willmaker from Nolo Press: 800-992-6656; $24.97.

Or, check out one of these books:

The Quick & Legal Will Book, by Denis Clifford. $15.95; Nolo Press; 800-992-6656.

The Complete Will Kit, by F. Bruce Gentry and Jens C. Appel III. 2d ed. $19.95 (paperback); John Wiley & Sons, Inc., New York, NY; 800-225-5945.

CHAPTER FOURTEEN

———————— $ ————————

Some Special Situations

The financial issues addressed in the previous chapters have applied to almost every parent. (If your child is just an infant, they will apply to you soon enough.) But this chapter discusses some special problems that don't affect all parents and that may arise at different points in your child's life. How to provide for a handicapped child after your death is an issue that concerns many families. Similarly, some parents want to know how best to manage the family finances when there are two sets of offspring, while other families have questions about what to do when a child comes back home, postcollege. All of these issues are important, but they may not pertain to you and your family particularly. If any of them do, however, please read on.

THE DISABLED CHILD

For parents of a seriously ill or handicapped child, the problems and costs of rehabilitative, custodial, medical, and educational services can be emotionally and economically draining. Disabled individuals, however, often qualify for certain government benefits, including health insurance, schooling, even institutional care. Before you attempt to bear this burden alone, be sure to look into the various sources of support and assistance—both public and private—that are available.

PRIVATE AGENCIES

Be it cerebral palsy, spina bifida, or mental retardation, there's an organization out there devoted to finding a cure for almost every disability and to help the victims and their families deal with it. While some of these organizations are little more than parent support groups, others are large, powerful national institutions that have wrought, through their lobbying efforts, a number of services and research funds for the disabled and handicapped. At the very least, these groups can offer practical advice on dealing with certain problems as well as information on available public support and how you might qualify.

PUBLIC SUPPORT

States often provide a variety of rehabilitative and custodial services. Sliding-scale fees are adjusted according to your family's income and how much you can afford to pay. (The number and type of services provided vary by state.) If you're eligible to collect Social Security, your surviving children may be entitled to "survivor benefits" if they're disabled. *Supplemental Security Income* (SSI), on the other hand, is for only the very poor. A person with less than $2,000 in assets who is incapable of earning more than $500 a month, for example, is entitled to SSI. In most states, a person who doesn't qualify for SSI probably won't be eligible for *Medicaid* either but may qualify for *Medicare.* Although it's often associated with the elderly, disabled folk who have been receiving Social Security disability benefits for two years or more may qualify for Medicare.

LONG-RANGE PLANNING

Of primary concern to most parents of disabled kids, though, is: What will happen when I'm no longer around to take care of my child? Unfortunately, disabled children sometimes must be supported their whole lives, often long after their parents have died. Making adequate long-range financial plans is crucial.

Parents should, if possible, develop a long-term savings plan (much like they would if they were saving for their child's college education). If it appears that the child will need assistance well into adulthood, parents can create a trust to provide for the child after their deaths. However, these trusts—actually any assets that you bequeath to a disabled child—can create problems if you don't know what you're doing. (Now's the time to get good financial advice. Look for an attorney who is experienced in estate planning, especially for families with disabled children.)

In most cases, you shouldn't leave any money directly to the child through either an ordinary trust or a will. State and federal programs generally cover basic medical and residential care, but only if the child has almost no money. An inheritance, even a relatively small one, can disqualify your child from receiving most government aid. The result may be removal from a group home, a special school, or some other program, for instance, that he or she has depended on for years, as well as loss of government-sponsored health insurance benefits. (Now, more than ever, you need a will. If you die without a will, your disabled child could inherit some or all of your estate, and may thus be disqualified from government aid.)

To avoid losing access to government programs and aid, you have to carefully consider your estate-planning options. Parents with modest assets often bequeath their estate to their healthy children and let the disabled child get government aid. In this case, you must specifically disinherit the disabled child in your will, or the court will generally assume that the child was simply forgotten and award him or her a portion of your assets anyway. (You might want to discuss, in advance, how the other children will provide any extras that the disabled sibling would need, after your death.)

Higher-income parents might set up a trust, which gives disabled children some extra funds after the parents die but generally allows them to still qualify for government aid. Your best bet may be a *special-needs* or supplementary-needs trust. Under this arrangement, the trust's funds are only allowed to be withdrawn for expenses such as clothing and recreation that are not covered through government programs.

Parents who don't have enough money to set up a trust can enter *pool trusts*, or master cooperative trusts, which let families jointly invest in a single trust that will eventually make payments to the children. The money is paid out on a percentage basis, according to the amount each family invested. These trusts are sponsored by groups such as the Arc of Texas and the Arc of Indiana. (To contact these groups, see "For More Info".)

You might want to make some other, less obvious arrangements, too. Disabled people often rely on their routines. Write these routines down—even if it's simple stuff like watching a favorite TV program at a certain time—so that when you're not around, someone else will know what to do. And pick someone to be your child's advocate, who will take over after you and your spouse have died. Even if your child lives in a government-sponsored home, things change.

Disabled persons always need someone on their side to make sure that their needs are being met.

THE BLENDED FAMILY

Money management is tough enough with just one set of kids. But finances can be a particularly explosive issue for stepfamilies—especially when there are two, or even three, sets of children to provide for. If you're a typical middle-class divorced family, there's probably never going to be enough money to go around. But you can take some steps to reduce the friction.

Some typical problems:

My husband always pays child support for his kids on time. But my ex is always late in paying support for our kids.

Alas, this is an all-too-frequent problem. But what can you do to get your ex to pay up, and on time? Start by talking to him. Explain that he's still responsible for providing some of your kids' support, even though you are now married to someone else. Tell him that you'll go to family court to have his wages garnisheed if he doesn't start paying up. If he heeds your advice, great. If not, you *will* have to go to family court. (This takes time and, if you hire a lawyer, money.)

Once the court issues a judgment against your ex (basically saying that he owes you support), it can get the money for you by garnisheeing his wages or his federal and state tax refunds or by putting a lien on his property.

My husband showers his kids from a former marriage with gifts we can't afford.

Some parents, especially those who left a marriage, feel guilty. So they buy their kids lots of fancy toys to make up for their absence in their daily lives. To get your husband to stop overspending, suggest that he spend more time with his kids rather than simply showering them with gifts. Remind him that your family budget is being stretched—and that you've had to cut back elsewhere—to absorb the costs of these gifts. If this doesn't work, set up a three-point system: yours, mine, and ours. Under this arrangement, you and your husband pool your money for joint expenses such as heat and the mortgage. Each of you gets some spending money—the mine and yours accounts—that you can spend as you wish. While this system won't stop your husband from spending, it should stop him from spending *so much*.

My husband's ex is taking him back to court for more child support.

Just when you thought you had it made: Your husband got a sizable promotion and the two of you finally have some disposable income. Not so fast. If your spouse's income has increased considerably since his separation agreement was signed, the court may well order him to pay his ex-wife more support. Generally, your income will not be considered since you're not legally responsible for supporting his kids. But it may be, depending on your circumstances and state laws. If your husband's current living expenses are reduced, for instance, because you pay a significant portion of the mortgage, a court may decide he can afford to pay his ex more support, if the kids need it.

To keep your income out of the battle, you may want to file future tax returns as "married filing separately." (You'll probably wind up paying more in taxes this way, though.) And you should keep your assets, such as a bank account, car, or house, in your name only.

My ex says she won't help pay for our child's college education.

If your separation agreement calls for your ex to contribute to your child's college education, she'll be legally bound to do so. If there's nothing in your agreement about college payments, however, you could always take her to court. But, depending on your personal circumstances and your state's laws, you might not win. Courts are sometimes reluctant to impose college payments on divorced parents because they don't impose a similar obligation on parents who are not divorced.

THEY'RE BACK!

Just when you thought it was safe to stop worrying about kids and money, your twentysomething children have come home to roost—again. One's looking for a job; the other is applying to graduate school. And they're both eating your food, talking on your phone, and just about taking over the family room and that extra bedroom you converted into a den. And you were worried about empty nest syndrome?

These days, lots of kids return home after college. Perhaps the job market is soft. Or they're unsure about the career they want to pursue. Some kids may be recovering from the breakup of a young marriage, with a baby in tow. Some may simply not be ready, or financially able, to live in an apartment on their own. Others may have a clearer grasp of their goals—starting a new business, for instance, or buying a first home—but they may lack the funds to do so. As the parent of an adult child, it's up to you now to decide how much support, if any, you're willing to provide.

Let's look at the pure money issue first. Your daughter wants to go to law school. Your son wants to start his own business. Do you give them the necessary funds outright—with no strings attached—or do you lend it to them?

All gifts are tax-exempt for the recipient (in this case, your child). But you, the donor, have some tax obligations, thanks to the Federal Gift and Estate Tax. In a single year, you can give each child up to $10,000 tax-free ($20,000 if both you and your spouse give the money jointly). If you want to give more, you can, often without incurring the gift tax. If your son needs $40,000 to fund his new business, give $20,000 to him and another $20,000 to his wife or another sibling who can, in turn, give that $20,000 to your son. Or, give him $20,000 in December. In January, the start of another calendar year, give him the other $20,000.

The trouble with gifts, of course, is that kids may not use your gift wisely or as you would like. A sibling may resent the fact that you bailed out his younger brother, and not him. In that case, you might want to consider a loan. While a family loan is a much more businesslike arrangement than a gift, the terms can be rather lenient. A loan made to your adult kids, for instance, doesn't necessarily have to involve interest; payment might be postponed indefinitely; or the debt could be forgiven eventually.

Siblings may still view a loan as preferential treatment, so keep good records. Fill out a promissory note, available at most office supply stores, with the child to whom you're lending the money. This document should be signed and dated and should state the terms of the loan. What is the interest, if any, being charged? When are payments due? Unfortunately, your child can't deduct the interest paid to you. And you must pay income tax on the interest that you receive. An interest-free loan—or what the Internal Revenue Service calls a "gift loan"—usually doesn't have any tax consequences unless the amount is substantial.

If you have no ready cash available but would like to help your daughter out, you could always cosign a loan with her. But keep in mind that you may be putting yourself at some risk. When you cosign a loan, you agree to be responsible for repayment of the entire balance of the loan should your daughter default on the payments.

Now let's look at the second issue: support. If your kids come back to roost for a while, should they pay you room and board? That depends on why they've come home and what your financial situation is. As a general rule, start with a nominal contribution, such as 10% of their salary, and work your way up. (By the way, the IRS doesn't require you to report such payments as rental income.) If your kid is a chatterbox, get him to kick in for the phone bill, too, or pay for a separate line. Obviously you can't ask Junior to pay up if he's not working, but you can ask him to do some chores around the house in lieu of payment.

Adult children—even those living under your roof—generally can't be included under your health insurance policy. Often, coverage stops when a child reaches a certain age or stops being a full-time student. (That information should be spelled out in your policy.) A child who doesn't have a policy through an employer may have to buy individual coverage. Choosing a high annual deductible of $1,000 or even $2,000 would lower premiums considerably. Under federal law, kids may be able to extend coverage under your plan for up to 36 months. (But they have to pay separately for it.)

Even if your 23-year-old is eating you out of house and home, you probably can't claim him or her as a dependent on your taxes. The exceptions: not working (or earned less than $2,550 during the year), or under age 24 and a full-time student for at least part of the year.

And now . . . the big question: How long will they stay? Some parents set a time limit, such as "You have six months to get your act together. Then I expect you to pay rent and your share of the utilities and the food bill." You could let them stay (rent-free) until they're ready to move out, but some adult children can get mighty comfortable letting Mom and Dad pick up the tab. And that may leave you drained, financially. At this point in your life, you're probably contemplating retirement, or, at the very least, that European vacation you put off years ago to pay for braces, private piano lessons, and soccer camp. How much more are you expected to shell out? That's up to you. But keep in mind that nowhere in the great contract of parenting does it say that you must keep on paying and paying and paying . . . until you've exhausted all of your resources. You owe it to yourself, your spouse, and your other minor children to balance expenses with your family's needs and the financial means you have at hand. It's okay to "just say no."

QUESTIONS AND ANSWERS

Q. My son was recently diagnosed as being autistic. Will my insurance plan cover the necessary therapy?

A. Not necessarily. Some insurers limit coverage through exclusions or qualifications, often denying coverage for anything labeled a mental health benefit or an educational or custodial service. When it comes to autism, for example, insurers frequently deny payment by claiming treatment is medically unnecessary, or an educational issue rather than a medical one. Where does that leave you? Thirty-one states act as insurers of last resort for residents who've been denied a policy in the commercial market or who have exhausted their own policies. In most states, though, the premiums cost at least 50% more than those of a standard-risk policy. The plans also may have lower maximum benefits than standard plans and may prohibit claims for preexisting conditions during the first 12 months. Depending on your state's requirement, you may be able to qualify for Medicaid.

Q. My daughter is thinking about graduate school. Will she be able to apply for financial aid?

A. In some cases, but it'll never be enough to cover the entire tab. Some graduate programs offer support in the form of fellowships, grants, and assistantships, but these vary according to the university and how well funded the government programs are that year. Medical and law schools, however, generally don't provide any financial aid, and the courses are so intense at these schools that students generally can't work part-time to offset some of the costs. If your daughter is thinking seriously about graduate study, she should expect to incur some loans or be beholden to you (if you're willing or able to provide such support).

Q. My husband and I both have two children from our previous marriages. We cover each of our respective children under our own medical insurance policies at work. Could we cover all four children under the same plan?

A. Probably, as long as your husband's separation agreement (or the laws of your state) don't prohibit his kids from being covered under your policy. If not, then compare the expenses and benefits of each policy to see which offers the better deal. Some points to consider: How much do you pay for coverage? (Some companies offer free coverage for employees but expect them to kick in for family members.) What are the individual and family deductibles? (Obviously, the lower the better.) Does either policy exclude coverage of a preexisting condition? (Not a great feature, especially if someone in the family has a chronic condition.) What is the maximum coverage on each policy? (The higher the better.)

FOR MORE INFO

If you're the parent of a disabled child, these groups can help:

The *Arc* (formerly the Association for Retarded Citizens) publishes a planning handbook for families and can help find local resources: 500 East Border Street, Suite 300, Arlington, TX 76010; 800-433-5255. The organization has 998 state and local chapters.

The *National Alliance for the Mentally Ill* also provides information and assistance to families: 200 North Glebe Road, Suite 1015, Arlington, VA 22203; 800-950-6264.

Exceptional Parent, a magazine for parents with disabled children, publishes an annual resource guide. A one-year subscription costs $32: 800-562-1973.

INDEX

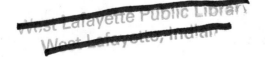